Stayin' Alive

SURVIVAL TACTICS
FOR THE
VISUAL ARTIST

Robin Hopper
**with contributions from business experts
and working artists**

Published by

krause publications
An F&W Publications Company

700 East State Street • Iola, WI 54990-0001
715-445-2214 • 888-457-2873
www.krause.com

Please call or write for our free catalog of publications. Our toll-free number to place an order or obtain a free catalog is 800-258-0929 or please use our regular business telephone, 715-445-2214.

Library of Congress Catalog Number: 2002113154

ISBN: 0-87349-571-3

Printed in the United States of America

I dedicate this book
to all artists who continually challenge my thinking
and make me realize the quality of life
and the importance of art and humanity in this world.

Acknowledgments

I wish to thank my wife, Judi Dyelle, for all her help in working on this book, from editing to photography, from philosophy to pragmatism and from creative thinking to criticism.

I also wish to thank the artists and authors who have joined forces in this project. Their input has been invaluable.

I wish to thank my secretarial assistant, Morgan Saddington, for her work in keeping my office on track, studio assistants Arlene Yarnell and Shana Watson, for holding the fort in the studio and showroom while I processed words in the office, and Britney, my dog, for taking me on daily walks that cleared my head and made me think. Many thanks also to my editor Barbara Case for reading between the lines as well as the lines themselves, and to acquisition editor Julie Stephani for believing in the need for this book.

Finally, I wish to thank all of my customers throughout the many years of doing business. Your support and patronage has perhaps been the most critical element in allowing me to do what I have done as an artist.

Robin Hopper
Victoria, British Columbia, Canada
September 2002

Table of Contents

Introduction

Although the content of this book primarily relates to the ceramic arts, the basic information, with its many personal viewpoints toward self-sufficiency and survival as a creative artist, is a paradigm, easily adaptable to the majority of the creative arts. Most problems and methodology of Stayin' Alive are much the same, regardless of media or discipline.

This book is about options and strategies for a life in the visual arts, independent of the world of education. It is a combination of my own personal experiences from 46 years of working as an artist in various disciplines, plus experiences from a number of other sources. Fortunately, nobody warned me that one couldn't make a living as an artist, so I always have! For the great majority of my working life I have been a potter, gaining many pragmatic viewpoints along with practical tips and tricks from working on four continents and setting up a number of studios in two countries. The book also draws from experiences of teaching seminars in survival tactics for artists. In addition to my own experiences on business development, self-promotion, pricing, and marketing, you will find chapters written by specialists on financial and legal matters, photographing your work, and gaining visibility. In addition, 19 other self-employed artists and sculptors offer their personal experiences in the field. While I can't guarantee financial success in your personal journey as an artist, the material offered in this book will help to develop a realistic attitude toward "making it" in a common-sense, sound, stable, and enjoyable way.

Chapter 1, Finding the Real You, questions who you are and the dreams you hold for a life and lifestyle. It then looks at the options, implementation, and some considerations to weigh before you begin buying equipment and developing an art business. Chapter 2, Learning to Be Businesslike, and Chapter 3, Pricing and Marketing, offer varying approaches for developing the business side of your brain. Chapter 4, Promotion and the Development of a Personal Image, addresses how you feel about yourself and your work and how to inform the general public of who you are and what you do. Chapter 5, Legal Considerations, is a brief look at legal aspects, from the type of business structure to contracts, copyright, death, and taxes. Chapter 6, Financial Considerations, looks at the financial end of running a business. Chapter 7, Achieving Visibility in the Art World, offers a magazine editor's expertise on what it takes to get published and how to get your work where it might be noticed. Chapter 8, Photographing Works of Art, offers tips and tricks of shooting images of your work for your personal reference and for possible use in publication.

Throughout the book there are several Biographical Sketches, short personal accounts by eight individual artists and six couples or partners, along with a selection of the work they do. Each has been selected both for diversity in the work and also the variety of personal journeys they have made to get where they are today. Between them, they offer 20 lifetimes of experience with at least 500 years of Stayin' Alive. These personal views are often funny, sometimes poignant, and always informative. Seeing how others have made their way as self-employed artists should give strength to those wishing to follow similar paths in life to achieve their personal dreams.

Go for it! There is little to lose and everything to gain!

Chapter 1:

Finding the Real You

Think Positive—It is an Amazing Antidote to the Negatives of Life!

Artist—1. A person who works in, is skilled in, or makes a profession of any of the fine arts, especially in painting, drawing, and sculpture, etc.—2. A person who does anything very well, with imagination and a feeling for form, effect, etc., a craftsman. Webster's New World Dictionary

What Are Your Personal Needs?

Although most people seriously underestimate their creative abilities and potential, not everyone can be an artist. Also, not every artist is cut out to be an entrepreneur. Being self-employed is a challenge that takes discipline and work.

Before jumping into the world of art or creative production, it is good to ask yourself a few important questions and seek out a few answers to determine your aptitude for this area of work. The lifestyle you desire, your income requirements and personal responsibilities, and your personality need to be reviewed before you make the decision.

Where would you like to live—city, small town, country village, rural area, in the mountains, or by the sea? Can you realize your dream locally or do you need to travel elsewhere? Is there good transportation? For many reasons some places may be conducive to your dream, others not. Where do you stand? Can you move to where you would like to be or are there reasons for staying put? Do you need to be near family, an education center, or have other ties or bonds to a specific space? Are you a loner or do you need others around?

Having a portable skill and being a creative artist is wonderful, but it's not all bliss. The opportunity to live a lifestyle where you are in control of its direction through creative activity is seductive indeed. Making art that is an expression of your being, enriches the lives of others, and contains a spirit of humankind is both a gratifying and humbling experience. The realization that you can affect a range of emotions through the creation of art using your mind, eyes, hands, tools, and raw materials is profound. The possibility of making an income from being creative and having fun is very real. Thousands and thousands of people are doing it to one degree or other. When it works, it is very enviable, but it doesn't work for everyone. It takes stamina!

What Do You Want to Do With Your Life?

People come into the widely varied world of the visual arts from a huge range of prior experiences, some through universities, colleges, and art colleges, and others from being self-taught or having taken a few classes somewhere. Some feel the compelling need to change both occupation and lifestyle. It is often said that at least 75% of the working population of North America dislikes what they do to make a living. I find it an extremely sad reflection on the value of life, to think that an average 40 to 45 year lifetime of work could be that distasteful, when options for a more fulfilling life are certainly available and attainable. At this point in history, when people are often seen as disposable, few jobs offer real security, and it is speculated that everyone will change jobs many times during their working lives, the concept of making a long-term living from a creative process is heartening, to say the least. The opportunity to make a personal human statement in an impersonal, sometimes inhuman, world is exciting. When you leave this life, the opportunity of leaving something tangible behind that says you have been here, enriching the lives of others, is satisfying indeed! More and more people are drawn to a more fulfilling path through life. The overriding similarity is that they all yearn to do something with their lives that includes using brain, eyes, hands, and heart to work creatively.

So what can you expect?

The life of an artist usually takes a tremendous amount of dedication, motivation, application, and intelligence. To be financially successful, it requires a strong work ethic. You should be prepared for quite a few tough knocks along the way as you hone your skills, and since artists are normally very sensitive, many who could easily make it on the quality of their work are often inhibited from doing so by the rigors and insensitivity of the marketplace. You have to develop a tough skin, hopefully without becoming cynical in the process. Whether city or country based, the working life of an artist is often isolated. It is difficult to be creative in a crowd, so prepare yourself mentally for this degree of loneliness.

One common problem is the lack of realization that to fulfill the self-employment dream, you need to develop skills beyond the artistic. Unless you are independently wealthy or are fortunate enough to have a wealthy spouse or partner, the process of Stayin' Alive through making art has to include some degree of business content to remain solvent and to allow you to grow in your work. Business itself is part of the creative act but it should be kept to a minimum, to develop a balance where pushing pens and filling out forms don't overshadow the more creative part of life. This book contains the basic information to make self-employment in the visual arts not only possible but very profitable, so that the artist can enjoy a personal lifestyle which is the envy of many, but the act of comparatively few. Those few are usually risk-takers whose values in life are not necessarily the almighty dollar but the desire for a quality of life that is rich beyond cash, with endless opportunities for personal growth and artistic expression.

Living in war-ravaged London for the first seven years of my life, I learned about business through osmosis by helping my parents in their grocery store. Although I knew I didn't want to be a grocer, this experience gave me the will to achieve what I wanted in life. My wife and I have a relatively simple life that is under our own control. Nobody can give us a "pink slip" or pull the rug out from under us in a layoff, firing, or company closure. We live by our wits and skills and the desire to make beautiful things that enhance the lives of others. We are part of a 10,000-year tradition of serving the needs of the community. We live on our terms in the way we feel life should be lived. This is the ultimate satisfaction of our lives. Life as an artist is no more insecure that any other working pursuit these days. It offers both joys and freedoms that other jobs don't. In these times of great and sudden change, where long-standing jobs are lost at the flick of a corporate pen, artists are probably more secure than most other working people. The insecurities of the past, when to be a self-employed artist was looked at as financial suicide, are no longer relevant. Being an artist is both acceptable and accepted, often honored, and with a lifestyle that is usually greatly envied. My wife and I live in paradise, play with mud, get great pleasure from the activity, give pleasure with the results of the activity, and still make a buck at the same time! Can life get much better than this?

What Are Your Expectations?

Achieving this lifestyle requires planning and, to some extent, disciplined control. It doesn't just happen. Knowing who you are, what your lifestyle needs are, and having the will to make it happen, are the basic structures on which you can plan your life. How much income do you need to live the lifestyle you want? In running business seminars for artists, I found that expectations range from just above the poverty line to $100,000 or more per year. While the upper level can be achieved, it will probably take some time to develop and will generally require additional income sources to do it. An artist with multiple discipline skills and trained in creative thinking would be well set for a larger income. In between the extremes of expectation, a wide range of possibilities exist. It is a matter of realistically looking at your life and setting priorities to allow yourself to achieve your desired future.

The pottery world is one of the easier places to develop a satisfactory income as a creative artist. For example, let's say a potter wants to produce a modest income of $30,000 per year. The annual studio overhead covering mortgage or rent, taxes, heat, light, telephone, automobile, materials and equipment, maintenance, insurance, and contingencies might be $20,000. If you add this to your desired income you will find that you have to sell $50,000 of work to achieve an income of $30,000. Using the simple example of a coffee mug (there seems to be an endless demand for coffee mugs!), which may wholesale for $10, it will take 5,000 coffee mugs to realize $50,000. This means making 100 mugs per week, or 20 mugs per day for 50 weeks. The complexity of the form and surface decoration, and the skill and speed of the artist control the output. Most working people put in an average of seven hours per day, five days per week, 50 weeks per year, or 35 hours per week. A skilled thrower can usually produce basic mug forms at the rate of between 10 to 30 per hour. On average, two hours of throwing would produce 20 to 60 mug forms. Additional time for handle-making and attachment, decoration, and glazing would probably triple the time of throwing. In 15 hours, or two days of consistent work, the basic weekly coffee mug quota would be met, leaving the other days to do other work, contemplate, or have fun! Although the coffee mug example may not excite the imagination of many, this could easily be changed to other objects that can be made and sold in reasonable numbers to produce the basic income needed. From my experience, it beats many other things you might have to do to reach this income, and you are improving your working skills the whole time. The more skilled you become, the better you are able to produce. The further removed your art is from the production example cited above, the more difficult it becomes to predict a reliable course of action. Much then becomes based on reputation generated over time. Overnight success usually takes years to achieve!

Success or failure in the visual arts depends largely on individual personality and a sound approach to business. A wealth of personal experiences on artists' survival tactics are given throughout this book by a variety of very experienced professional artists. They offer the student or person wishing to make a change in their life concrete methods they have used successfully. As a general rule, students in colleges or universities get very little or no introduction to the business of being an artist and the process of survival after leaving the hallowed halls of academia. At the time of writing this book, fewer than 30% of institutions offer business programs for artists. Hundreds of MFA and BFA graduates in ceramics come from schools every year. There are very few teaching jobs available. The skills learned in school are seldom geared to self-employment, so the great majority fall by the wayside, often with a huge student debt load. People who wish for a change of working life and lifestyle are perhaps a little better off. At least they know what they don't want to do, so the desire to achieve a more personally satisfying lifestyle becomes paramount.

Chapter 2

Learning to be Businesslike

Whether you are selling ceramics, silk blouses, serigraphs, shoes, or sausages, the basic tenets of small business are more or less the same. A product is made or purchased, priced and marked up for the retail market, and then sold. From the sale of goods a profit should be realized. This allows more product to be made or purchased, and the cycle continues. Many artists seem slow to realize that once you enter into selling your artwork, you become a businessperson or entrepreneur as well as an artist. The better a businessperson you become, the more your art and business will likely thrive. The ebb and flow of a basic business approach carries through to the interaction with other businesspeople such as store and gallery owners, consultants, collectors, and curators, as well as the retail buying public. It is of primary importance in developing and sustaining a successful small studio practice.

You may be the absolute best in your field of artistic endeavor, but unless you are visible, can sell your work, and maintain a business, you will have great difficulty surviving as an artist. Even though it may be a challenge, it doesn't have to be onerous. If being businesslike means the difference between Stayin' Alive and the alternative, you owe it to yourself to learn to be businesslike. It can and probably should be part of the creative approach to life; a means to an end, but not an end in itself.

Some of the text in this and other chapters will require you to get a local viewpoint, as legal, financial, employment, and taxation issues differ from state to state and country to country. The text will suggest that something may be of concern. Local questioning and individual research will provide applicable answers. Laws change even within small distances. The city where I live has 11 different municipalities, each with a unique set of bylaws. Something you may be encouraged to do in one area may be illegal a block away in another jurisdiction! Check out what might affect you and your business plans.

The paths to your personal dream are far more numerous now than ever before. With flexibility in the artwork you make and an ear to what people may be looking for, you can diversify your product in many ways. To optimize your production and produce the best potential income, you need to be conversant with different styles and technologies. Specific processes, surface effects, and colors are often popular today but out tomorrow. The number of interested buyers becomes exhausted and moves on. Many artists change their product line by 30% per year. Having a very narrow range of product severely limits the sales potential. Times change, so products should too! A little like investing in the stock market, awareness and ability to deftly change course makes for greater revenue.

Starting a business in the visual arts is normally a gradual affair, from small beginnings that might go from being just out of school or having a hobby that begins to pay for itself. It's good to move slowly when starting out because there can be many pitfalls along the way. Finding your marketplace is often a complex problem. Sometimes participating in art or craft shows is a good start. Develop a mailing list to inform clients of upcoming events or shows. If you are working from home, make sure it is legal to either make or sell there. If you need to expand your home operation, is it allowed? What are your local bylaws?

When I started my first studio in England in 1962, I had a young family, so I needed to make things that would have a sound potential for sale. As a student I had sold a lot of work, so I had the self-confidence to think I could make it work. I had saved enough money from other jobs to make it possible to switch to my own studio and remain solvent for at least six months. I opted to make functional production pottery, as there is always a market for it. I designed and made a small range of what I felt I could reliably produce on a repeat basis. The pieces were photographed and put into a professional looking portfolio.

I worked out the wholesale price structure (see Chapter 3: Pricing and Marketing) and researched which stores and galleries around the country handled the sort of work I planned to do. There were enough outlets to split into three circuits in different stages. In stage one, I contacted each outlet in one circuit to let them know I would be in their area at a given time and made an appointment to see them. In stage two, I acquainted them with my work through the portfolio. If they were interested, I had samples in the car. If not, I didn't waste their time or mine and moved on to the next business on the list. In stage three, I brought in samples of my work, discussed the product, took orders, arranged a deadline for delivery, repacked the samples, and left. In a few days I had enough orders to keep me busy for the next two months. I went back to my studio, made the work, and delivered it on or before the promised date, establishing reliability. I then did the same thing on the second circuit, followed by the third. In six months, I had established retail contacts throughout the country. In the next six months I repeated the process to develop a basis for annual production.

At the same time I opened a small showroom in my studio and quickly realized that selling retail was a very good thing. I tried to do as much retail business as possible (see Chapter 3: Pricing and Marketing). The retailers were impressed by a businesslike approach, unusual for artists at the time, and my studio thrived from the beginning. This works very well in a relatively small geographical area where there may be many outlets, but in North America, other avenues should likely be approached. In North America, this small localized selling has generally been superceded by participation in juried art fairs or craft shows, where the audience for your work comes to you. Buyers from across the continent come to major juried events like these, which have established a reputation for showing high quality work. With a combination of good merchandise, an attractive sales booth, effective salesmanship, and good luck, artists may take enough orders or sell enough work to develop an interesting and comfortable living. Many artists take enough orders to last the whole year. After a number or years of having my studio in England, I moved to Canada. I took a similar approach in researching potential retail clients, as well as being represented in a gift show for retailers. In six months I had contacts in 35 stores and galleries across the country. This was my starting point and quickly built to where I could confidently stop teaching, giving me 30 extra hours a week and allowing me to concentrate on being a full-time studio artist.

My advice in developing a business is to keep it simple, be organized, reliable, persistent, flexible, and always creative. Unreliability and procrastination were once considered the hallmarks of a creative person; nowadays this doesn't generally fly!

It is difficult to make a realistic business plan in the arts, but if you need to borrow money from a financial institution to achieve your goals, you will almost certainly have to make one. It will be a speculation of business development for a period of one, three, or five years, depending on the financial institution. The basic cost of equipping a studio can easily be found by researching what is needed. Used equipment may often be found. Estimating the business cash flow is usually little more than an educated guess, as business in the arts can fluctuate with the economy and seasonal cycles. In my business I have found that when the economy is buoyant, people buy more one-of-a-kind, higher-priced collector items. In a slow economy most sales are the lower-priced, more functional items. There are bound to be times when compromises have to be made, times to tighten your belt and times to loosen it. You should never compromise your work, just take a realistic look at possible new directions. As long as artists don't start out with heavy debt and extensive costs, they are usually flexible and manage to "go with the flow" better than others who may have greater expectations.

Becoming an Employer

As your business grows, you may wish to take on other workers, apprentices, or assistants. Make sure it is allowable under the local bylaws for your particular workplace. It may be too expensive to hire somebody outright, as employee costs can be considerable, requiring an hourly rate of pay, holiday pay, pension plan, taxes, unemployment benefits, and worker's compensation. Many of these costs are specified by federal or state labor departments.

There are a number of approaches for employing people.

1. Instead of a salary, offer board and food and/or education with possible studio privileges.
2. Have the apprentice pay the master (you). This is often a more realistic learning situation at a considerably lower cost than an educational institution. This is difficult but not impossible to find or negotiate.
3. Don't pay the apprentice until they prove adequately useful.
4. Pay by the piece. In this scenario, the assistant receives an agreed amount for each piece made.
5. Pay an hourly rate for all work done.
6. Obtain government grants, which are sometimes available to train new employees.

Employing people to produce your artwork sometimes works extremely well, but beware of personality conflicts and keep a firm grasp of who is the boss.

If you don't enjoy the business part of your business, it usually pays dividends—both fiscally and sanity wise—to get someone to do it for you. If you don't like to deal with sales, packing, shipping, and cleaning, hire somebody. A good bookkeeper or accountant can often save many more times their cost by giving you more productive time to do your artwork, rather than playing with numbers, pushing pens, and completing forms (see Chapter 6: Financial Considerations).

It is always a good idea to have a savings plan for future growth, development, and contingencies. Even when you are a new art business and probably not making that much income, putting up to 10% into savings can build a nest egg for later life or problem times. As with any form of insurance, the earlier you start, the more effective the savings. Disability insurance is certainly something you should consider.

Computer Literacy

One of the most important things you can do for yourself in a small business is to become computer literate. The computer is an indispensable business tool that assists you in inventory control, sales, marketing and promotion, and even product design and packaging. If you lease a computer, the whole cost can be written off over time. Software applications are available for almost anything. Accounting, spreadsheet information, databases for address lists and glaze recipes, Internet for research and contact development, and the amazing capabilities for graphics give flexibility and control to the artist in ways never imagined before.

Increasing Your Business As a Partnership

You may consider taking on a partner right from the start, or later as your business grows. Costs, profits, losses, and workload can then be mutually worked out, making sure that you have contracts legally drawn up, signed, and witnessed to safeguard all parties (see Chapter 5: Legal Considerations). A lawyer or accountant or both can advise you should you consider incorporation.

Incorporation is a legal process by which a private corporation is developed from individual proprietors (see Chapters 5 and 6, Legal and Financial Considerations). When the income produced through a sole proprietorship or partnership gets high enough or requires the payment of personal income taxes (a variable from state to state and province to province), taxation may be alleviated by forming a company of incorporation. Effectively, the owner(s) of the business becomes an employee of the business and both the company and the employee combined pay taxes at a lower rate than the individual would. The higher the income, the greater the savings. Besides offering potential tax advantages, incorporation is also a protection against litigation. If the company is sued, the personal assets are protected. For example, if you have an incorporated company, it makes sense for you to rent to the company the property that houses it and any major equipment. Should the company be sued for any reason, the property is just rented from you and is therefore not in jeopardy of loss should the case go against you. A legal incorporation is drawn up by a lawyer, often but not always in conjunction with financial advice from an accountant. The name of the company may be followed by various words: Inc., Incorporated, Limited, Ltd.

With larger businesses and partnerships there is often a considerable financial advantage to being incorporated. Incorporating your business can provide great benefits in its efficient operation and can limit the possibility of personal financial loss in the event of a business failure or any form of litigation brought against you. Incorporation can provide great peace of mind.

Biographical Sketch
Tom and Elaine Coleman

Written by Tom Coleman
Photos by Tom Coleman

Tom and
Elaine Coleman.

In the fall of 1964, after a short stint in the Army, I enrolled in the Pacific Northwest College of Art in Portland, Oregon, to study painting. It was there that I met Elaine, who was also studying to become a painter. At that year's student Christmas sale, Elaine and I had our latest work on display and heard comments like "very interesting," and "good sense of color." I noticed that people were leaving our area and making a mad dash to the dark end of the school where the clay people worked, where excitement, joy, and laughter prevailed. Later, the same potential customers walked back past the painter's area with their arms full of pottery and various clay objects. It was at this point that Elaine and I became interested in clay, not because it sold well, but because people were having such a great time making and selling it.

Our first ceramics instructor was a very proper elderly woman who had been teaching ceramics forever. Everything was fired in an electric kiln and we were allowed only a quart of blue glaze per semester. We sprayed the glaze on the pieces, then meticulously scraped the overspray back into the jar to be reprocessed. After a year and a half, Elaine had to leave school and get a job due to lack of funds. I continued on with school by working as a part-time janitor there. By my second year into the ceramics program, I was bored stiff. I started to research the Art Museum Library to find out more about the clay world. This is when I began to think of ceramics as an art form and not a craft. In my third year the school hired a crazy man to run the ceramics department. His name was Bill Creitz and he actually made a living as a potter. This totally changed my ideas about clay. Bill shared his great

throwing skills and knowledge about ceramics. We made up five gallon buckets of glazes that weren't blue and burnt up the electric kilns by firing them to cone 10 and reducing them by throwing mothballs into the peepholes. At this point I was completely in love with clay and Elaine! In the middle of my third year of school we were married. I was awarded a full scholarship to finish my education at the Pacific Northwest College of Art.

The same year I became an apprentice to Bill, who brought me to his studio to work. He had electric wheels, gas kilns, and an old Navy dough mixer for making clay. I became very familiar with this mixer. One of my jobs as an apprentice slave was to mix a ton of clay a week for Bill to use and to sell to other potters in the area. Also during this time Elaine and I rented a tiny house in Portland. We set up a small bedroom as a pottery of sorts and purchased a 12" by 12" 110-volt electric kiln, which would hold eight mugs at a time. If they turned out, we took them to a little hippie gallery in Portland called The Green Mitten. If the mugs sold we received 80% of the $4 price.

In the summer of 1968 I graduated from art school with a fine art degree and was given more responsibility in my teacher's studio. I was now mixing glazes, firing kilns in reduction, and throwing a lot of my own pots. It was at this point that Elaine quit her job to help me in the studio. My grandmother, who raised me, developed lung cancer and moved in with my mother, so Elaine and I rented her old 700-square-foot house that had a garage we could someday use as a studio. It was at this time that Elaine and I decided we were going to be studio potters for the rest of our lives together.

Porcelain platter. Hand-thrown and altered. Multiple crystal matt glazes with wood ash. Fired to cone 10 in reduction. 23" in diameter, 3" thick. Tom Coleman.

Porcelain thrown and altered vase. Green matt glaze with wood ash. Fired to cone 10 in reduction. 16" tall x 11" wide. Tom Coleman.

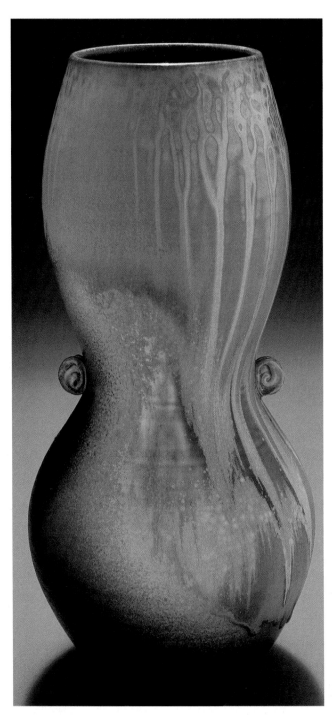

Porcelain hand-thrown vase. Multiple crystal matt glazes with wood ash. Fired to cone 10 in reduction. 16" tall x 6" wide. Tom Coleman.

Incised lizard and leaf teapot with green celadon glaze. Fired to cone 10 in reduction. 10" high x 12" wide. Elaine Coleman.

Our parents thought this was the dumbest decision anyone could make. How could you survive as an artist? We were just young and naive. We never thought we couldn't make a living off our work because we were totally in love with clay and the lifestyle that went with it.

In 1969 I was abruptly weaned from my teacher's studio because of my reluctance to design my own forms and my ability to emulate his. What a mess this put us in. No studio set up, no wheel, no kiln, no clay or glaze materials, and barely enough money to pay rent. Thank God for Elaine's father, who liked me and had the ability to construct and design equipment for cheap. He helped us build an electric potter's wheel and gas kiln out of scrap materials. We scrounged enough glaze and clay materials from school and potter friends to start producing work. Almost all the pottery being produced at this time in the Pacific Northwest was stoneware. I decided to try throwing porcelain because it would provide me with more of a canvas for my brushwork. The clay supply companies didn't handle a good porcelain clay because there was no demand for it, so I started mixing a porcelain clay body by hand and wedging it on the cement studio floor. This changed my direction in clay and from that point on, I continued using porcelain and doing surface decoration.

The pottery scene in Oregon in the late 1960s and early '70s was primarily functional, so we already had a leg up because of working for Bill who was the best! Elaine and I started producing a line of plates, mugs, casseroles, and teapots that we took to a commercial pottery in Portland called Pacific Stoneware in hopes of selling them. To our relief they loved the work and took all the pieces. We jumped for joy—"Our first real paycheck. Let's get drunk and call our parental doubters." After this shot of encouragement we decided we might be ready to approach some local galleries and enter some shows. The galleries didn't provide us with enough income so we started doing some Pacific Northwest fairs and I got a part-time teaching job at Portland State University and the Pacific Northwest College of Art. Between the three, we were able to purchase our first house in Portland

and produced two children, Jason and T. R. We didn't have a studio at this home so Patrick Horsley, Don Sprague, and myself formed Atlas Clay Studio in a warehouse in the old part of Portland and worked together for about a year and a half.

Feeling the need for our own studio space, Elaine and I bought an old farmhouse on the outskirts of Portland. It had a great barn that we turned into a workspace, gallery, and clay mixing facility. During our 15 years on the farm in Canby, we became studio potters again. Elaine primarily kept the kids out of my hair when I was working and took care of the business paperwork. She also started working on her first incised pieces, learning the hard way. When both kids became school age, Elaine began working full-time again in the studio. Over the years our combined work slowly became recognized and collected in the United States.

Porcelain hand-thrown and altered oval vase. White matt glaze with wood ash. Fired to cone 10 in reduction. 13" tall x 9" wide. Tom Coleman.

In 1976 we received a phone call from John Nance, a writer who was well respected and knew our work. A publishing company based in Portland wanted him to write a series of books on Oregon artists. John decided to start with clay because he was somewhat familiar with it and had a small collection of Oriental pieces. Elaine and I were the "chosen ones." The book was published in 1978 and opened many doors to out-of-state shows and workshops.

During the latter years in Canby, I wanted to break away from the restrictions of decorated porcelain. Frank Boyden, Nils Lou, and I formed a partnership called the East Creek Anagama, which was a funded project to build a wood-fired kiln in the Japanese tradition. I felt that the wood-fire process using porcelain would be interesting and give me the opportunity to experience a more natural way of approaching clay. Although in the early '80s, wood firing wasn't really appreciated by the public in the Pacific Northwest, it was and still is a great passion of mine. I got some incredible pieces out of that kiln and over time realized I dumped some wonderful work over the bank due to my unwillingness to accept the slightest imperfection. Like an old Irish friend of mine once said, "You got to loosen up man!"

In 1985 I was invited by Mike McCollum, the head of the ceramics department at the University of Las Vegas, to teach a summer session. Wow! Sunshine and blue skies every day. I felt energized. It was then I realized how depressed the rain and gray skies in Portland made me feel. I was invited back again the next summer and after that the family made the move to the southern Nevada desert. We bought some property outside of Las Vegas and built a home and studio. While working on the two buildings, for extra income Elaine worked as a gallery director at a new local gallery and I was hired part time at UNLV.

The kind of pieces we had been making in Oregon were not readily accepted in Nevada, simply because they had nothing to do with the area. Elaine invited me to have a one-man show of new work at the gallery. This was the beginning of my series called "The Test Site." The Test Site Series started off as a joke but soon developed into an intriguing approach to my work and new environmental surroundings. The new body of work was one-of-a-kind, cone 6, bright neon colors with dry desert crackle earth surfaces over sculptural forms. The show was a success and photos of my pieces were published throughout the United States. We were invited to many shows and private collectors began to contact us about the new work and our prices soared. With this new success, Elaine quit her job at the gallery and refocused her attention on incising porcelain and I quit my job at the university.

In 1995 we opened Coleman Clay Studio and Gallery in Las Vegas. This was done to develop and educate a new group of people interested in throwing clay. The school and gallery proved to be very successful and filled a need for people in the community interested in clay outside of the university system. After seven years we decided to turn over the business to a clay supply company, and we are now enjoying being studio artists once again. We each have our own jobs. I throw Elaine's and my pieces, Elaine incises and does the bookkeeping. We both price and pack work to be shipped off. Our sources of income today are mostly derived from sales to private collectors, workshops, lectures, glaze books, and a few galleries.

During our 38 years in the business, we have never felt the need for an assistant or an agent. We like our privacy, with just the two of us working together in our studio. Elaine and I have traveled to give workshops and lectures throughout the world and have met some wonderful potters. We wouldn't change a thing. We have a great life!

For information on purchasing work or books by Tom and Elaine Coleman, e-mail Elaine at celedonqueen@aol.com or write them at 1003 Santa Ynez, Henderson, NV 89015, Web site: www.tomandelainecoleman.com.

Incised frog and leaf vase with green celadon glaze. Fired to cone 10 in reduction. 10" tall x 5" wide. Elaine Coleman.

Incised porcelain crane bottle with dark blue celadon glaze. Fired to cone 10 in reduction. 9" tall x 7½" wide. Elaine Coleman.

Incised porcelain lizard vase with green celadon glaze. Fired to cone 10 in reduction. 8" tall x 7" wide. Elaine Coleman.

Biographical Sketch
Malcolm Davis

Malcolm Davis.

When first contacted about contributing to this book, I thought, "Sure, why not? I've got a story to tell!" But on further thought, I realized that I have little to share in terms of how to start and run a business and I certainly have no pointers on how to be a success. But I do know something about "stayin' alive," so I want to share a part of my journey as a way of offering an alternative model. For those of you who feel you don't have a hare's chance in hell, this one is for you. And the message is: Don't give up.

I write this in the year I turn 65 years old. There is no way that I would have ever dreamed or planned to celebrate this milestone making pots. I had hoped to retire as a banker or an academic, ending my career with a gold watch and a healthy annuity.

Born and bred in Virginia's Tidewater, I knew nothing of clay or handmade pots. Our dishes were Lenox! In 1959 I graduated Phi Beta Kappa with a Bachelor of Science degree in mathematics and headed to Hartford, Connecticut, to begin life as an actuary. My hope was to climb the golden ladder to the executive suite and rule Hartford as an insurance magnate. But when introduced to my cubicle of dusty ledgers, I was out of Hartford in less than a week!

What to do? Well, I entered Union Theological Seminary in New York City, of course. What else? The life of a bishop would surely be more interesting than that of an insurance magnate. But within weeks I was in jail, arrested for picketing a Woolworth's store to protest their policy of segregated lunch counters in the south. So much for the bishopric!

I did indeed graduate from Union Seminary, married my seminary sweetheart, got ordained in the United Church of Christ, and entered the campus ministry. Judy and I became deeply immersed in the movements for civil rights, women's rights, social justice, and the movement against the war in Southeast Asia. We were radicals. We intended to change the world, to end racism and sexism, militarism and imperialism, to stamp out homophobia and chauvinism. We were committed to building a new society. But the old society was after us. Our home was bugged and my office bombed and we ended up on Nixon's infamous enemies list of citizens to be rounded up in a national emergency.

It was then that I discovered clay. It was an accident. I thought I was going to a lecture! But I left that "lecture" a changed man. I was 45 years old when I left the campus ministry to become a full-time studio potter. I tell this story to encourage those who get a late start; to say that it's okay and that the life that went before will inform the clay and may well create work that is better, at least more mature.

I dared to leave my career with no technical training or preparation. I had no BFA, no MFA, and very little technical aptitude. I had never even fired a gas kiln. Technical knowledge is not a prerequisite. It helps, but if you are not so inclined, you can still make good, honest pots. When you run into problems and need to figure something out, the information is out there. Learn it when you need it, as you go along.

I have no background in art or design; in fact the only art class I ever took was in high school and I flunked it! The scar remains, and I will always consider myself a potter rather than an artist. I believe that art school is not necessary and might well dilute or distract the passion.

I have learned that the important thing is to make honest pots, personal pots that come from your heart and hand, pots that speak your voice, sing your song, have your handprint. That comes from the love of the material and the passion for making. It requires a lot of hard work and discipline, but a degree is neither required nor necessary.

I have very little business smarts. I was not attracted to clay as a way of making a living. I had already had a successful career. I just wanted to make pots. But in order to be free to make pots, I had to learn to market my work and pay my bills. I have survived by living simply and surrounding myself with good friends and good pots. My studio is in an unheated, uninsulated hovel with a dirt floor gloriously perched atop a mountain in north central West Virginia.

Looking back on this journey, I think the most essential ingredient for survival has been passion—love for the material. Determination, commitment, and discipline have all helped. But the power of that passion gave me no choice but to pursue the dream and take my chances.

It would not have lasted without a supportive wife and partner who continues to work to make it possible. The birth of this passion had its roots in strong teachers, role models, and mentors: Cynthia Bringle, Karen Karnes, Mary Nyburg, and Mikhail Zakin. The strength to continue in the face of disasters, including the loss of my studio by fire, has come from friends who actually bought those early pots and continue to do so. And, of course, the earth binds us potters to one another; so gratitude must be paid to my community of fellow makers who have stroked me when necessary and challenged me when needed.

Fortunately there have been those unexpected, unearned, and untimely sparks that come from a little luck and occasional good fortune. For me it was the discovery of the shino glaze. It was purely accidental. I knew nothing of it at the time. I had lost my studio and had a residency at Baltimore Clayworks. I had a successful line of white tableware—lots and lots of white pots. They sold well, but the soul was in need of help. When I unloaded that first shino pot, my life was changed. That was over 15 years ago and I continue my eternal, obsessive search for those illusive molecules of trapped carbon.

We potters like to think that it is our energy and vision that mold the clay into forms that we desire and determine. Au contraire! In the end, it is just the opposite. It is the clay, the living earth, that transforms us. None of us potters could stay alive without the power and possibility of the clay that seduces and sustains us. How delicious to be making a living by doing the very thing one loves. And, it has never been boring!

Malcolm Davis, 2322 19th St. N. W., Washington, DC 20009, e-mail SHINOm@aol.com.

Photo by D. James Dee.

Personal Teapot.
6" high x 5½" wide x 4½".

Shino Vase. 9" x 4" x 4".

Sushi Plate. 2" x 9".

Teapot.

Biographical Sketch
Catharine Hiersoux

Catharine Hiersoux

Photo by Richard Sargent.

My exposure to clay began in the early 1960s when the craft movement was just beginning. In fact, we were all just discovering what this material was about. With no set rules or standards and little or no markets, we pioneered our way, risking and exploring without expectations. Probably a blessing, as there was little to lose and much to gain.

I continued my clay work at UCLA, later marrying my high school sweetheart. Arne was a leader, committed to pursuing a creative path—art, architecture, business, whatever, a veritable risk taker. I knew intuitively that he could take me on a great ride, so I hopped on (the feminist movement had yet to happen!).

We began a life centered around family and art. It appeared relatively balanced in spite of the social and political turmoil of its time. Our major struggle was always financial. Arne had committed to being a painter, working odd jobs to pay the bills. I started my involvement with clay, occupied with childcare and running the household by day, making pots and teaching at night. We shared a studio, quickly learning that clay and oil paint don't mix. We needed to have separate studios. We balanced family concerns with our creative projects, enjoying what we were doing and gaining knowledge and confidence with each event.

As our needs for space developed, we went looking for live workspace to put family and art together. Across the street was a brick building, a frozen meat locker. We put a bid in on this 8,000-square-foot space, offering half the asking price with the condition that the landlord remove the refrigeration equipment. He countered and said we could have it for that price, but we had to do the work. We agreed on the terms, borrowed $5,000 from my mother, and launched into a 10-year project of gutting and rebuilding this site. After nine months my studio was operational and we were able to move in. I was making a range of porcelain plates and vase forms. We built a large gas kiln. As I was already making large plates that filled the bottom, my question was how to fill the top. I started making a series of tall forms.

One day I received a call from the director of a museum in Los Angeles, who told me about a luncheon in Washington, D.C., and asked if I could make 12 place settings to be ready in three weeks. For ceramics that is not much time, but for me it was even more critical as the size of the kiln required three weeks' work to fill. This was my 15 minutes of fame, though it lasted much longer. This acknowledgment was a major turning point in becoming a career artist, largely due to the power of the press. The success that every artist dreams of had taken my somewhat balanced life and catapulted it into high profile. Now I had to get serious, take responsibility, and be professional. I needed a brochure, high-quality slides, and employees to help with the studio work. I had to spend money to make money, with funds we did not have, putting pressure on the family. I continued to do art fairs, especially the ACC shows, taking orders and returning to complete them. Usually I had at least one helper. Many combinations were tried with employees but the most workable was trading studio space and materials for work.

Invariably glitches happened. In taking orders and promising to deliver at a specific date, I was challenged to not only produce a quality product but also to be accountable. Mistakes happened, like losing the copper reds, the mainstay of my color palette. It was embarrassing to have to notify stores that I needed more time. Three weeks' work was lost, and funds for the mortgage payment delayed as a consequence. Success was all around but there was also failure. Learning how to manage a business became traveling in the fast lane. There were invitations for exhibitions and workshops.

Vase. 17" tall.

The gallery activity was increasing as well as wholesale orders and later lecture invitations. There was so much attention that doing it all and taking care of the family was difficult. It was a lot of pressure. The good news was that I was finally making a living with my work but our collective projects were high intensity, like being in a whirlwind.

I worked with classical shapes and beautiful colors, especially copper reds. I loved the color and found an audience that responded. One day I opened the kiln and there was a beautiful copper red vase. It had become a signature piece—a form about balance between vertical and horizontal forces, resting precariously on a narrow base. It was later named the Earthquake Vase. As I lifted it out of the kiln, I sensed something was wrong. It had split in half. The glaze was too tight, the walls too thin, the Yin/Yang balance broken. In addition, it was the symbolic expression of the end of our partnership, as Arne had died six months earlier of a brain tumor. The expanded metaphor was that this form, the shape of my life, was no longer viable. The neck was too narrow, the form too tight, the color too pretty. No longer could I maintain the pace. The rhythm had to change. My life had shattered apart but I began to restructure the pieces. As the work changed, the forms dictated a new firing process, leading to wood firing, opening many adventures and broadening my vision of clay. I dismantled the large gas kiln in the studio and rebuilt it as a wood kiln. I learned with each firing, making many mistakes. Gradually a new vision of work developed.

As the next phase of this journey began, there were significant changes. I reduced the production and wholesale sales. The work was more one-of-a-kind, not conducive to repeat orders. The gallery in the house studio became the main outlet. The process of learning wood firing led me to focus more on process and less on product. It is also communal and spiritual.

From the ashes we learn to understand our process, its rhythm. We learn to embrace the dangers, its rigor, and we learn to trust in the magic, the magic of the fire. The journey continues.

Catharine Hiersoux, 437 Colusa Ave., Berkeley, CA 94707, e-mail: hiersoux@earthlink.net.

Tea Bowl. Wood fired. 4" tall.

Rock Vessel. Wood fired. 13" tall.

Photo by Richard Sargent.

Fist Bottles. 20" tall.

Chapter 3:

Pricing and Marketing

Pricing Is Purgatory, Marketing Is Mandatory

For almost every artist, novice or seasoned expert, the act of putting a value on the results of your talent, time, and materials is probably the worst part of being creative. In the beginning, artists tend to give their work away to friends and family. After they have exhausted the potential recipients of these donations, or realize that in order to continue they need to buy more materials, the prospect of "going commercial" raises its ugly head and they have to come up with a price or value for the marketplace. Establishing this is a complex issue!

Most artists usually have little or no idea of the precise cost of producing a work of art or craft. There are just too many variables. At first, the artist may be slow and tentative, with talent just emerging. The time required to produce art is usually fractured, with things that have to be done at different stages in the process. Some stages may take seconds, while others may take hours. For example, almost all pottery, one of the most technical art forms, has at least a dozen stages in its development—raw materials inventory control, clay preparation, weighing out, throwing or other making method, assemblage, drying, fettling or surface cleanup, packing kiln and bisque firing, unpacking kiln, glaze making, glazing, glaze cleanup, decorating, packing kiln and glaze firing, unpacking, cleanup of glazed ware, pricing, and storage. If complex third-or-more-firing decoration processes of overglaze enamels, gilding, or cold processes such as sandblasting or acid etching etc. are done, the number of separate stages can easily reach 24 for one object. It is almost impossible to put a cost on this mix of activities or calculate the time involved. Some stages would be deemed highly skilled, while others could be done with little or no skill.

Talent is priceless—the greater the talent, the more valuable the work. Depending on the art form, the material costs may be either very high or very low. In jewelry they are high, in ceramics low. It is also very difficult to establish an accurate materials and processing cost on a per-object basis. Some arts are low-tech/high time, while others are low-tech/high material cost. Almost all are labor-intensive. Simply put, **Cost = Talent + Time + Materials.**

In pottery-making a simple formula for general costing to establish a wholesale price can be done as follows:

Cost of production (for wholesale price)

10%	materials (average)
10%	firing cost (average)
30%	wages—skilled design, materials research, development, making the work
30%	wages—low-skilled or nonproductive work such as unloading supply trucks, mixing clay, cleanup jobs, inventory control, telephone calling or answering, correspondence, driving, talking to people, doing promotional work, filling forms and dealing with government bureaucracy, packing and shipping. (In short, anything that keeps you away from productive time. Realistically speaking, in a one-person studio, this works out to about three out of every five days spent in production.)
20%	overhead—rent or mortgage, interest on business loans, insurance, bank charges, light, heat, phone, automobile, office supplies and equipment, computer, printer, desk, chairs, filing cabinets etc., studio equipment, clay mixer, pugmill, wheels, molds, slab roller, benches, chairs and tables, shelving or ware carts, kilns and kiln furniture, etc.
100%	total cost

This basic formula establishes the cost of anything produced. A similar breakdown can easily be made for a retail price, whether in your own selling venue or through a store or gallery. When you have an idea of production costs, you can add the profit margin to develop the income base you feel you need to establish the lifestyle you want. Final income is basically dependent on how you market your work—consignment, wholesale, agency, retail, or commission.

Even with the above information, it is still difficult to establish a basic price for your work. A process that worked well for me when I was a neophyte studio artist was to visit craft stores and galleries and make a list of the artists who did work along the same vein that I was planning to do. I then made a list of the prices that a variety of their objects were commanding. Next, I made a graph with the artists' names down one side and the objects along the bottom. I filled in the prices of the objects by each artist and calculated the average. That became my retail price, which I divided by two to establish the wholesale price. Putting my price bang in the middle meant that I wouldn't be either under- or overpricing. This method served me well when starting up in England in the late 1950s. In 1968, when I moved to North America, the costs of living and production were quite different and I did the same thing. As a result, I've been surviving well for 46 years.

There are other methods for establishing prices found in other books, but I haven't found them to be any better, more informative, or more accurate than the above. Establishing a price for very personal, exploratory, or nonproduction-based work is quite different. It is mainly whatever the market will bear, and is established through different criteria. Reputation, credibility, and longevity tend to be the guidelines. Well-established artists with a distinctly recognizable style of work are obviously a better bet for the collector than a newcomer. Reputations (other than negative ones) don't usually come either easily or quickly! Gut reaction to the object and its qualities is probably the most reliable indicator of its quality and value.

Marketing

The decision on how to market your work depends as much on your lifestyle choice as on your desire for visibility. Some artists like the bucolic existence of a simple, uninterrupted life in a country setting, while others feel the need to be city-based in the race for high visibility and, hopefully, high potential income. The former might sell his or her wares in country markets or by regular wholesale, whereas the latter usually needs well-established galleries in high-traffic areas with high-income clientele. No matter where you stand in this equation, marketing is done in one of a number of ways—consignment, wholesale, agency, commission, gallery, or retail. Each has both positive and negative aspects.

Consignment

Most people start selling their work with consignments. It is a way of both testing the waters and being tested by the marketplace. Unfortunately, it is also where many people remain.

The positive aspects of consignment selling are the opportunity for first exposure to the buying world and developing that important first group of buyers. Consignment is a good way to sell larger and more personal speculative artwork that may have a final price tag that inhibits sales.

Most galleries have consignment arrangements with artists, even the most established and recognized ones. When selling by consignment, contracts must be in place for the mutual protection of both the artist and the gallery owners (see Chapter 5: Legal Considerations). Galleries can build the reputation of the artist through exposure of the work to collectors, public institutions, and architects.

The negative side of consignment is that your work is often used as backup stock by stores who may purchase from more established artists but consign with newer ones. If they have their money tied up in your work, they are more likely to put it in a prominent spot. If not, your work may be consigned to the stock cupboards until other work is sold out.

In my opinion, it is best to cease consignment selling just as soon as it is feasibly and financially possible. If you are fortunate enough to develop a good long-term working arrangement with a reputable gallery that is knowledgeable about the medium you work in and that cares about both you and what you make, it might be wonderful. However, there are many unscrupulous art dealers out there and the history of selling art is littered with broken and illegal deals and bankruptcies. The artist is merely a pawn in a high-cost game where your money is tied up and theirs isn't. Even the law doesn't adequately protect artists. In the worst-case scenario, a high-visibility gallery owner can usually afford high-priced lawyers, whereas the artist generally can't!

Wholesale

In wholesale selling, the artist establishes a price that covers the cost of production plus enough profit to continue working. The price should cover business development and allow future investment, including savings. Once established, this price becomes the basis on which the artist sells. Purchasers (usually stores and galleries but sometimes restaurants and anywhere else artwork is sold) then mark up the price to cover their costs and give them adequate profit to allow development of their lifestyle. The markup is usually 100% (50% of the retail price) but may be much more. If the retailer thinks they got a bargain price for work that is worth considerably more, or they have an upscale market venue, they will likely sell the work for much more than double their cost outlay.

The positive side of wholesaling is that somebody believes enough in what you are doing to invest in it for the purpose of resale. It also gives you upfront or 30-day payment, usually a blessing for the starving or financially-challenged artist. Good retailers who sell your work often do a great job of building your reputation in a venue that you wouldn't want, or couldn't afford, to work in, in a place that may be across the country or in another country altogether.

The negative side is that you usually need high-volume production to make an adequate income. This often leads to low-quality, quick-to-produce work. Artists often begin to resent the wholesale purchaser, thinking that the artist bears all the costs and the purchaser makes all the profit. The reality is that the purchaser has money tied up in work that may not sell quickly and if they are in a good retail venue the rental costs may be phenomenal and their other overheads may be similar to yours plus the added costs of staffing.

Agency

This is the process of selling through an agent or sales representative who usually sells your work to a retailer, making his income from the commission that he has worked out with you.

On the positive side, for some artists with a large volume of production, this is often the only practical way to get your work out to the widest possible market. Good sales reps establish a network of merchants to carry your work, some in specialized markets like public gallery and museum gift stores and some in general retail centers.

The negative side tends to be that selling through an agent either increases your workload or considerably raises the retail price of each object. Agency selling is not recommended for the small-scale worker or the artist doing speculative, personal, or large-scale work. Most often in an agency sale, the agent takes the order for the work, passes it on to the artist who makes it, and sends the finished work to the retailer. The retailer pays the agent, who then takes his commission and sends the remainder to the artist. This way the agent is sure to get his commission!

Commission

Artists in all media produce commissioned artworks. A commissioned work is anything done for a particular client, designed according to the client's requirements. Commissioned projects can be anything from small-scale jewelry to huge murals, sculptures, or installations.

Working through private or public purchasers, the artist usually designs and produces site-specific works in conjunction with architects or interior designers. This allows the artist to produce larger and more complex work that can usually fit into the gallery situation.

Sometimes gallery owners will arrange a meeting with prospective clients for an agreed-upon fee. Some galleries specialize in this area of marketing. The artist retains the copyright on all works unless foregoing it by prior arrangement. All commissions, particularly higher priced ones, should be arranged with a mutually acceptable contract signed by both parties.

Gallery

Galleries are normally either commercial (in business for profit) or public (where the reason for their existence is primarily educational). In a commercial gallery the objective is to show work, usually through exhibitions and, hopefully, generate sales for the artist and commissions for the gallery. Exhibitions are expensive to mount and the costs to both the artist and gallery may be high. Contracts outlining who is responsible for what expenses eliminate misunderstandings. From the artist's viewpoint, costs will include making the body of work to be exhibited. Sometimes weeks, months, or even years may be required to produce quality exhibits. Finished work may need to be photographed early for publicity purposes, media information, invitations, and posters. The gallery owner provides premium space, public relations, and sales expertise. Commission rates and responsibilities for opening night costs are worked out between the parties.

Positive aspects of commercial gallery shows include the opportunity to expose a selected range of work or a particular direction that the artist is currently exploring, the possibility of a number of sales in a short time, the extra visibility from public relations, the addition of information to your resumé, and the opportunity to get feedback on your work in a serious way.

Negative aspects of commercial gallery sales include tying up your time and money for a considerable period, putting many eggs in one basket, and experiencing a large degree of pressure to produce. A large amount of trust is required on both sides.

In a public gallery, the major objective is to show the artist's work in an educational setting. Normally, the work is not for sale. Although sales may be arranged as a side issue, they are not the primary reason for the show. The gallery arranges the exhibit with the artist, sometimes provides a curator and catalog for the show, looks after the installation, exhibition, and dismantling, usually pays an artist's fee for the rental of the exhibit, keeps track of potential buyers, and other interested parties, and occasionally arranges a subsequent tour to other public galleries.

Positive aspects of this type of exhibition include reputation building, the opportunity to produce a body of work without being overly concerned with sales, the artist's fees received, and the possibility of a catalog for both current and future use.

Negative aspects are minimal, but include the time and cost of producing the work, the work being tied up for a considerable time, and a high degree of pressure to produce. It is usually considered a great honor to be invited to exhibit in a public gallery.

Retail

From an income-producing viewpoint, you will get the highest return on your investment of time, talent, and materials from direct retail selling, either from your own gallery/showroom, art and craft fairs, or special shows and events created to specifically exhibit and sell artwork. The retail price is usually double the wholesale. For the extra income, there will be extra outlay in the form of creating, staffing, and stocking your gallery.

Retail spaces for artists run the gamut from specially designed galleries with the latest in electronic gadgetry, lighting, video, music, computers, bank card machines, and all the trappings of a sophisticated gallery aimed to attract the high-end buyer to the messy annex of a studio where customers have to blow off the dust to see the work and the proceeds of the sale go in a glass jam jar. Wrapping is newspaper and you do it yourself. Between these extremes is a wide range of possibilities that should be considered when setting up your retail center.

When the showroom fully reflects the quality of the work and the artist's pride in its display, it can become a destination for buyers of all means. Clients really enjoy meeting artists and having the opportunity to ask questions about the work. They then become informed and make good ambassadors for what you do. Good customer service pays off handsomely!

As usual, there are both negative and positive aspects to retailing your own work. Negative aspects include the upfront cost of setting up a gallery or traveling exhibition booth for art fairs or trade shows, packing and shipping, the interruption of your time and subsequent loss of production, and never being quite sure where the next mortgage payment will come from! The time interruption can easily be solved by employing someone to take care of sales and run the sales outlet. It usually takes some time—two to five years minimum—to learn the pattern or seasonal variation in sales. Much will depend on the location of the venue and how much advertising or other visibility developing processes you do (see Chapter 4: Promotion and the Development of a Personal Image).

The positive aspects are found in greater revenue, control of stock, uninfluenced personal decision making in product development, interaction with buyers or collectors, and immediate response to new works.

It is usually best to think of the retail part of your studio as a separate entity to make it easier to apportion expenses correctly. On paper, the studio sells the work to the showroom at wholesale prices and the showroom marks it up to retail price for sale. It may sound complicated, but it is quite simple, and makes inventory control much easier.

It generally takes time to establish a personal gallery, so other selling methods are conducted to cover the interim period. Much of your best promotion comes from word of mouth. When the business takes off it becomes a more reliable indicator of market trends and what people may be looking for, allowing for quick product development and market testing.

Sometimes artists think they double their profit by selling retail. Depending on the costs associated with selling retail, the profit margin can be much greater. For instance, an object sold to a retailer for $50 will likely be marked up to sell at $100. The initial wholesale price of $50 covers all the production costs plus a moderate profit, perhaps 10%. Your own gallery costs or the costs of selling through trade and art shows are usually much lower than the costs born by retailers who have high visibility retail space, staffing, and overhead costs. Typically they make a profit of about 10% to 15%. Your own gallery should cost no more than 40% of the retailer markup, eventually giving you about 70% total profit (60% + 10%), as opposed to the 10% from selling wholesale. The added income allows you to either make less work to achieve the same income or have more time. This, in turn, is likely to encourage you to make a higher quality product—possible with the extra time and cash—and develop a higher value product that makes getting visibility easier. It is a "Catch 22" in reverse: more cash allows more time to create better work, which receives greater attention, sells for a better price, and brings in more cash!

In direct retail shows there can be considerable costs for booth space, but they often serve the artist very well. Checking with other artists often gives a good idea of the potential of any given show. In general, proportionate costs are considerably higher than your own gallery, but participating in a show may introduce your work to a huge audience. Keeping an address list of buyers and interested parties can become the basis for home galleries. Many artists make a lifestyle of production in the fall, winter, and spring months and juried art fairs in the summer months, often traveling around the country to superior events. If there are a number of artists living in close proximity, annual or semi-annual studio tours might be a good possibility. Irregular home shows for two or three artists can also offer possibilities. Always check with local municipal governments regarding bylaws and business permits for this sort of event.

A number of artists living and/or working in a fairly close geographical area can easily pool resources for advertising and development of studio tours. Several individual artists can be represented on one brochure, which might include street addresses, phone numbers, e-mail addresses, and Web sites for future sales potential. There might also be a map of studios and any other relevant information. The example shown is from a South Vancouver Island group of artists. Studio tours to artists' workplaces, homes, and gardens are very popular events for the buying public, who usually greatly enjoy the opportunity to meet the artists whose work they collect. Studio tours are an important opportunity for the artist to make personal contacts.

Trade shows are just like selling regular wholesale but with the huge advantage of a captive marketplace of high-power buyers. It is a case of high-cost promotion with high possible return. Many artists get enough orders at trade shows to keep them in production for the next year. It is a good way for your work to be seen along with other high quality work. It is a tough and tiring marketplace but many thrive on it.

In the long term, your own lifestyle desires and requirements for income dictate the way you should attempt to develop your business. There are many roads to success. Choosing the right one for you will take time, observation, decision making, and luck.

Stinking Fish Studio Tour brochure.

Biographical Sketch
Susy Siegele and Michael Haley - A Dialogue

Susy Siegele and Michael Haley.

Photo by Mike Haley.

"I love making pots so much I would make pots just to give away if I didn't need the money."
–from a workshop with David Davison in the early 1970s

Mike: The secret to our survival is a combination of dogged determination and dumb luck. We have always tried to maintain a lifestyle that is hands-on (cheap) and tried to keep our operating expenses under control.

We started our clay careers in the mid-1970s. It was a unique, magical time in American society—a time of naiveté and idealism, and of openness to new ideas and old cultures. A time when one (or preferably two) could live cheaply and tread gently on the land, while trying to figure out how to make a living doing something that was creative.

Susy: The thing that can't be duplicated is our great good luck. How can you advise people to "have good fortune"?

We were both studying pottery when we met and began producing work together in the early '70s. Our intention was to follow the advice of songwriter John Prine: blow up our TV, move to the country, build us a home.

We had read about a village in Japan in which all the people made pottery for half the year and farmed the other half. That sounded so idyllic we decided we would do it, too.

Pottery was to be an adjunct—a way to bring cash money to the homestead. We never imagined ourselves as great artists or considered that we were creating memorable work. We loved clay and felt free as birds to make anything in any size or clay body and fire it in any kiln that was desirable or available. And what a serendipitous time it was! Everyone we met loved our work, whatever it was.

People wanted things that were natural, handmade, organic, real. They wanted to dream about the lifestyle Mike and I were going to try to pull off. We made pots and sculptures, built kilns, grew vegetables, hiked and camped, all without any concern for time clocks or accountability. We sold our work cheaply or gave it away. We made lots of work. We also lived like college students when we were beginning our first studio: no children, no phone, no TV, no running water.

There's no denying that luck plays a big part in the success or failure of everything, and that we have been extremely fortunate. We still have both sets of our parents, and although they thought we dressed goofy and were hopelessly naive, they were always tremendously supportive of our endeavors.

We were lucky to be living and learning about clay at a time in history when we could see examples of clay art from thousands of years ago right up through time to where we were, working out of a little old farmhouse on the rolling plains of Texas. No other culture had ever had the advantages we had, so how could we possibly fail?

Then the Corps of Engineers condemned us. They had decided to build a lake to supply Dallas with water. We were only renting the old farm (we had voluntarily upped our own rent from $50 a month to $75 when we moved our clay studio from the house into the old barn), but we had been there for several years and had developed a bit of a clientele who would drive out from nearby cities to buy our work.

This was 1977 or so, and cheap old farmhouses had become hard to come by anywhere near Dallas, plus who knew when the Corps would decide to dam up another river, so we decided to move further out into the country. We had fallen in love with the Ozarks for their beauty and the down-hominess of the people who lived in the hills. They were certainly not pretentious, and we liked that. Plus land was cheap and abundant. We would

"Blynken's Blanket." Slab and extruded teapot and tray. 1988.

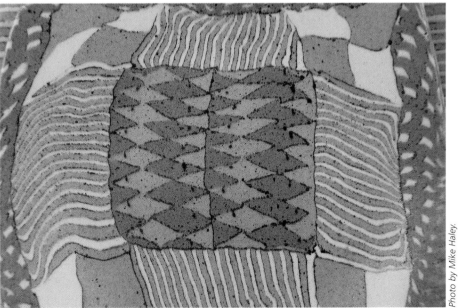

Detail of "Blynken's Blanket."

homestead; build our own energy-efficient studio and live in a loft above it, making improvements as we could afford them.

The main drawback to moving up into the hills was leaving our market behind. There were no good craft shows very close, so we knew we would have to develop a wholesale market if we were to be able to make a living selling pots.

We can't say enough about our teacher, J. Brough Miller, of Texas Women's University in Denton. Male graduate students were allowed into the program! We enrolled under Miller and got more life education for our dollar than ever a state university intended to give. Miller was a red-haired, freckle-faced grump who had studied at Cranbrook under Maija Grotell, and was as gruff as hell. Gruff Brough. He made big, strong thrown pots. And, with come-alongs and winches, he bent and welded steel plate into enormous, organic sculptures. He was genuine. Everything sounded like a thesis topic to him. He provided no answers. Figure it out for yourself. Nobody out there in real life is gonna do it for you. Be self-reliant.

In those graduate student days, Miller would come along singing and stub out his cigarette in our slip bucket. He would taunt us into making real work, challenge us to grow up, give us projects so abstruse we're still working on them 28 years later! The value of a strong character in your life, who acknowledges you and believes in you is vital. Perhaps Mike and I provide it for each other. But you can't say enough about the good luck of finding a real teacher.

After we left Miller, we built kilns. We moved bricks, tons of bricks, and built lots of kilns. We worked hard. Expected nothing. We were long and lean. We threw pots; we did shows. We lived on an old farm three miles up a dirt road, 25 minutes from town. Our shop was in an old barn. We had dogs and goats and chickens. We had a garden. We lived near a college town with an art community. Who could have asked for more?

After the Corps of Engineers condemned the place, we had to move, so we bought a piece of mountainside in northwest Arkansas. We built a building that housed the pottery shop on the first level, and we lived upstairs. We were making the transition from selling at craft fairs to producing for the wholesale market. We had a baby. We hired people to help with clay mixing and increased our production. We paid employee taxes. We went to the Dallas Market. We went to San Francisco and West Springfield. We had another baby. That's when we rented a building in town and hired more help.

It was an old cabinet shop. It had been for sale for ages. Just sitting there empty. We talked the owner into a six-month lease. It was right on the highway, half a mile south of town. We built a big wood-burning kiln, fired it once, and decided that we should have an open house. We invited other craftspeople to show work at the opening, and the basket makers invited their insurance agent. She bought the building. We had our opening and our closing on the same day!

Faced with the prospect of moving the pottery back into our house, we decided to build a new shop on our property. The wholesale business was rolling. We paid as we went and never borrowed to build our shop. For a short period before the new shop was finished, we did have to move back into the house with three employees, a school-age child, a brand new baby, and an endless production schedule.

The new shop had no amenities, and I ran the carpenters off before they put the trim on anything. I had to go to work! A rainwater cistern and hand pump were added later, as were a clay storage and mixing area. We heat the whole shop with a little woodstove and have lots of tall windows and high ceilings. They let your spirits soar; this we absolutely believe in.

We continued to grow, eventually having four assistants. We refined our colored clay patterns and taught our assistants how to make them. Susy had become a full-time manager and most of her energy was spent making sure each person in the shop was doing what he or she did best according to their particular strengths and our production schedule. It was a very frustrating time for me; I realized that my personal studio space was now smaller and much less private than it had been when I was a grad student!

It seemed like all I was doing was loading and firing the kiln. We had developed a bastardized wood/gas kiln that we fired for about 24 hours at least once, and sometimes twice, a week. It required eight to 12 hours of stoking, plus wood gathering and preparation. (These were things I preferred doing myself. They were kind of my meditative time.) And then we unloaded, sanded all the pots, and started getting ready for the next firing.

What happened to us then, as a byproduct of the wholesale business, was becoming larger than ourselves. We always had good relations with our employees. But when money and time and the quantity and quality of productive work one is willing or able to accomplish becomes an equation, a new element enters into your life. Mike and I became more and more involved with shows and sales and travel to and from them, and computerizing and photographing and printing and advertising and employee taxes and benefits and on and on! We had become a business; the joy was evaporating as we began to feel that we weren't necessarily in charge of the work we were creating.

Our denouement is fairly interesting. Do you have

"*Broken Rainbows.*" *Teacups, 4" high. 1987.*

Photo by Mike Haley.

the right to dismantle your own business? Our workers didn't think so. We discussed and negotiated and weaned our business over a period of three years. The first year, we did no trade shows and added no new wholesale accounts. Two of our workers teamed up, bought a kiln, and began exploring other kinds of pottery.

The second year we produced as a group for two three-month sessions. Mike and I spent the other six months making pots, scheduling orders, and doing shows, as well as gardening and being parents. Our workers built kilns, took classes, and began to make their own work.

Year three we worked the same three-month-on/three-off schedule, eventually weaning from each other. Three of our workers are making and selling pottery, sometimes collaboratively, sometimes not. Their success varies as their lives get pulled in different directions.

Making functional pottery provides a double challenge of creating innovative and aesthetically pleasing work, while at the same time, making sure each piece works the way it's supposed to. We had our first concept of creating a "line" of dinnerware in about 1980 while preparing for our first wholesale market. The American Craft Council was helping craftspeople and gallery owners get together through their show in Rhinebeck, New York, and when they scheduled a show in Dallas, we applied and were accepted.

We were so green. But so was nearly everyone else, so we got away with it. Our booth was a conglomeration of thrown work, slab-and-extrusion constructions, and colored clay. Our first buyer explained to us how to sort the pots in our booth so that the distinct types of work could be understood separately. He liked the colored clay and made an order. At that point, I realized that the little book of receipt tickets was not what we needed for writing an order, so I ripped a page from my sketchbook and that first wholesale order became the guide for what would become our order forms.

The next year we had price lists, and the year after, photographs and information sheets. We were having to learn about product photography and how to prepare our stuff for the printer. It was a forgiving time—you could learn things as you went along. I think now you have to jump into that wholesale market in full bloom.

Inertia: A body at rest tends to remain at rest; a body in motion tends to remain in motion. - Newton's First Law of Motion. How do you work when you're not inspired? Well, it happens. Sometimes you have to pretend you are happy until your psyche catches up. I usually find that a new idea will emerge after a low, unproductive period. You can't force it, but sometimes you have to use the calendar and the clock, jumpstart yourself, and make work that is dull and uninspired just to get some momentum going in your studio.

Differences

Our whole history is concerned with working out our differences. How to create art from your heart, run a business, build a home, raise children, when you both have conflicting opinions about most everything, but you are both too involved to let up. It's tough. If I presumed to have advice for someone, the best advice I can think of is this: make do. Don't expect things to be better than they are. Do things in as simple a way as possible, with as low-tech tools as possible. Upgrade your space and equipment as required, but don't go overboard with stuff you don't need. It always pays off to be generous of your time with your community. Finally, do all of it because you love your work. This is probably the only subject on which we both agree.

Susy Siegele and Michael Haley, RR#5, Box 775, Huntsville, AR 72790, e-mail: susymike@madisoncounty.net.

Hollow rock cairn. 22" high. 1999.

"Winged Reflections." Tea set. 1986.

"Woven Window." Platter, 15" x 15". 1991.

"*Trap and Tassili.*" *Dinner set. 1997.*

Colored porcelain gargoyle. 12" x 18". 2001.

Anne Hirondelle,
2002.

Photo by Janet Knutson.

"I'm either going to law school or I'm going to make pots," I said to a colleague at the feminist social agency I was directing. "Remember," she advised, "you can always eat out of pots." On the first day at orientation I knew that law school was not for me, but it took a year of briefing cases, reading tortes, and attending lectures before I found the courage to follow my intuition.

At 28 years old with a B.A. in English and an M.A. in counseling psychology, I enrolled in a beginning pottery class and spent a year at the Factory of Visual Art in Seattle. The next fall, 1974, I entered the B.F.A. program at the University of Washington, my formal introduction to the art/craft world. Robert Sperry showed me that the vessel could be a legitimate and outstanding form of personal expression. Aware of the plethora of potters, I asked him if he thought there was room for more. "There's always room at the top," he said.

In 1977 my husband Bob and I moved to Port Townsend on Washington's Olympic Peninsula, where we bought a small house on two city lots. The configuration of the existing outbuildings determined my initial studio space. I equipped the 10 by 14 foot room with an electric wheel, extruder, two worktables, a wedging table, some shelves, and a small wood stove. It was tight, but I was thrilled to have a space of my own.

Eager to establish myself as a production potter, I did my first firing in the fall of that year. Ironically, it wasn't until I was on my own that I started learning; work was the real teacher. After two and a half years of production stoneware, I explored raku-fired vessels and drawings, as well as painted clay construc-tions. I experimented with scale, learned to sketch as a way of searching for and clarifying my ideas, and began to see my work as pure form.

When I returned to making stoneware vessels in 1984, I had found the beginnings of the work that was truly my own, the work I continue today. I am drawn to the vessel as an abstract form and metaphor for containment. Earlier pieces were based on a wheel-thrown cylindrical shape to which I added lids, handles, spouts, and bases. More recently, I combined thrown parts to create core shapes where I continue to work in an additive fashion. Solid and hollow extrusions are cut and manipulated. Coiling enables me to make elements—openings, lips, collars—that are not necessarily round or symmetrical. My goal is to combine these techniques to create a seamless whole. My glaze is unusually high in soda ash. Since 1984 I have varied the oxide combinations as well as firing temperatures and atmospheres to achieve a range of patina-like finishes—unadorned surfaces that complement my forms.

My small studio space served me for 17 years until architect Jim Cutler offered to trade a new stu-dio design and working plans for two of my pieces. Bob and a friend built the structure, which attaches neatly to the existing buildings; it looks as if it has always been there. After having worked in close quar-ters for so long, the 375 square feet felt luxurious. Surrounded on two sides by my perennial garden and vacant lots on another, my studio is light, spacious, and inviting. I love being here with my office, work-space, and glaze room all under one roof. An adjoin-ing shed houses the 50-cubic-foot downdraft kiln I designed and built for both bisque and glaze firings.

"Yinpod." Stoneware. 8¾" x 12" x 12". 2001.

Photo by J. Robert Gibeau.

It still fires as consistently as it did 25 years ago.

My new vessels were first exhibited at the Seattle Northwest Craft Center in 1985. Roger Schreiber, who has since photographed virtually all of my work, offered to take images in trade for a piece of work. When I finally got the nerve to submit them to *American Craft* and *Ceramics Monthly*, both magazines called immediately. *American Craft* published a "Profile" piece with two images in 1986. Later that year, *Ceramics Monthly* asked me to write a feature article that appeared on the cover of the summer issue. This national exposure resulted in calls from galleries and collectors. Since then, I have been represented by galleries throughout the group shows. I also sell directly from my studio if an individual visits independently of one of my galleries.

When we moved to Port Townsend, Bob and I made a conscious decision to live modestly so he could work part-time and I could work full-time at my art. Asked if I support myself with my work, I usually answer, "Yes, but not necessarily in a style to which you may want to become accustomed." I stay alive by working hard and living simply. I enjoy traveling to attend my gallery openings and to teach workshops. For the most part, however, I enjoy being in the studio and in the garden. I work alone; I belong to no groups or organizations. To make my way and to sustain my place in the art/craft world, I rely on the strength of my work as well as the intrinsic meaning and pleasure I derive from the process of working. After 25 years, I remain amazed and grateful for this life of clay.

Anne Hirondelle, 2255 Haines St., Port Townsend, WA 98368.

Photo by Roger Schreiber.

Capo. Stoneware. 21½" x 10 x 7". 1999.

Carabao. Glazed ceramic stoneware. 6" h x 16" w x 11" d. 2000.

"Ocarina." Stoneware. 9" x 12½" x 11". 2000.

Biographical Sketch
Peter Powning

Peter Powning.

Photo by Beth Powning.

What I like about what I do is that despite the frustrations and risks of self-employment, I am engaged on a daily basis in activities and concerns that matter to me. I have, I tell myself, control over my own working life. If I feel like it's getting out of control, I'm in a position to change that. It's not always easy answering to oneself, but at least there is no question about whom I answer to ... at least as far as my work is concerned.

I've made my living since 1972 as a what? Object maker? Certainly as a potter, but also making sculpture, architectural commissions from tables to fireplaces in a wide range of materials but chiefly in clay, cast and slumped glass, cast bronze, and lately steel and stone. I thrive on experimentation, transformation by fire (raku, bronze and glass casting, saunas!), and the pursuit of creative ideas. I like challenges.

My working life is always in flux. I used to think that once I'd found the formula for a successful career, found the groove, it would be easy sailing. Fat chance! I now realize this whole business is about flux and change and one's ability to adapt and be flexible with changing times and changing interests, not to mention aging body parts. I've learned from some mistakes, sold others, and seem to find some impossible to resist repeating frequently. If I'm not screwing up every now and then, I'm not trying hard enough, not taking enough risks.

I set up my first studio in 1972 in a derelict grain shed on an old hill farm in New Brunswick near the fabled Bay of Fundy in Canada. I was 22 years old at the time and was done with university, married, and keen on settling into a simple life making pots, growing our own food, and being connected with the natural world. Thirty years later my wife and I are still on the same farm, informed by the same ideals and have a swordsmith son and his wife living next door with our new granddaughter. Sounds idyllic and romantic, and in many ways it is. Yet there have been many difficulties, hard times, and dissatisfactions along the way. We have often felt isolated from other artists. My decision to make pots for a living was based on the assumption that making sculpture wouldn't provide enough income to live on. I think I was right about that, but alongside the pottery, I always had some sculptural project on the go. Most of what I make now is sculpture.

When I started out we had visited many studios. I thought it would be a good idea to pattern my studio after an experienced person's setup. I still think this is a good idea. You quickly get a good sense of what appeals to you and what you can manage by seeing how other people have gone about setting up. It was particularly useful to visit young potters who were recently established since they, by necessity, had simple, affordable studios.

I now have three studio buildings incorporating a foundry, forge, metal shop, wood shop, glass slumping/casting facilities, arrays of computer-controlled kilns and annealers, a studio gallery, storage space, shipping/packing room, and office. Guess where I spend most of my time? The office! It's very hard not to move from simplicity to complexity as your career progresses. Staying in one spot for over 30 years has led to the accumulation of horrendous quantities of overburden. I understand why the remains of ancient civilizations are found many feet below current ground level. I'm not sure what to make of this state of affairs. I love having the ability to produce the work I do mostly on site, yet I yearn for a simpler working life. So my advice would be to keep things simple and don't blindly embrace expansion, debt, and complexity. I have talked myself into this situation because facilities in this rural area for casting metals, working glass, and other operations are not available locally. My overhead, however, is daunting.

Making a living from one's creative passions and skills always involves compromise. I could have made a living doing something else to support my artistic preoccupations but that seemed perilous as well. I managed to balance the production and sale of pottery with my sculpture making, expanding the time I spent on sculpture until it has pretty well taken over. It was an evolutionary process that happened in fits and starts over about 30 years. Along the way I've tried marketing my work in almost every conceivable way, from selling it out of our very rural house to wholesaling, retailing through co-op and partnered galleries, catalog sales, Internet sales (a nonstarter), wholesale and retail exhibitions, and the now ubiquitous craft fairs. All had their time and place. My main advice is to be persistent, flexible, and creative. I now make most of my living selling on consignment through half a dozen galleries, doing solo shows with them periodically. I'm also regularly represented in museum and gallery group exhibitions and do private and public commissions. It can all seem overwhelming at times, so keep it as simple as you can. The benefits of supporting yourself through your creative output outweigh the difficulties. The real rewards are not financial.

Working with my hands gives me a sense of connection not only with others doing similar work, but with generations of predecessors who lived by the skill of their hands. Those of us who produce work by processes we try to understand and control, by hand from beginning to end, maintain a vital link to an essential part of our humanness. It is an aspect of our species that has evolved over millennia and that many who live typical contemporary western lives are quite distanced from. For those people, we form a link to that heritage. I believe there is an innate human ability to recognize and appreciate the handmade, the object imbued with the power of the skilled and thoughtful hand.

Peter Powning, Powning Designs Ltd., 610 Markhamville Rd., Markhamvile, New Brunswick, E4E 4H3, Canada, e-mail: ppowning@nbnet.nb.ca, Web site: www.powning.com.

"Penumbrium." Raku and bronze. 12½" high.

Photo by Peter Powning.

"*Lunarium.*" *Glass, bronze and raku fired clay. 26" high.*

Lichen Reliquary. Ceramic and cast bronze. 9" high.

"Moonlight on Branches." Glass, cast and bronze. 57" tall.

Chapter 4

Promotion and the Development of a Personal Image

Promotion and personal image are the engines that drive the business machine. How you present yourself to the public has a tremendous effect on your bottom line. Although thought of by some as crass, personal image development can make the difference between success and failure. The most important thing is that you have confidence in yourself and your work, which gives others confidence in you. Potential buyers are often timid about making decisions and need the additional benefit of promotional material to feel comfortable in making a purchase, especially a large purchase.

In any business, the better you look, the more people will be intrigued with what you have to offer. The higher the quality of the work, the better the promotional material needs to be. Get a high-end printing job done. If the promotional material contains photographic images of your work, they should be professional quality (see Chapter 7: Achieving Visibility in the Art World, and Chapter 8: Photographing Works of Art). If the image doesn't accurately show the quality of the work, it won't do you much good. In the short term, people may be interested but if the merchandise doesn't match the hype, the long-term will likely fizzle.

All promotion is basically advertising, and may vary from simple information on paper to complex information on screen—from the business card to the video clip. Cost-wise, promotion can go from quite inexpensive to a significant percentage of your budget, depending on how, what, and where it is done. Doing your own artwork in a computer graphic program will significantly lower production costs while giving greater personal freedom in the design. Whatever you say about yourself, in whatever format, should be truthful, enticing, accurate, and to the point.

Portfolios and Resumés

Historically, the artist's primary promotional tool is a portfolio of images of work in the form of either photographs or slides, along with a resumé outlining his or her personal history, educational journey, and exhibitions done along the way. It often contains listings of where the work may be seen or purchased, details of public and private collections that may hold the work, and publications in which the artist is represented or has personally written for. Although it is still a valuable information tool, at the beginning of the 21st century, this form of portfolio is largely being superceded by electronic media using Web sites and CD-Roms for greater and more immediate access to information and images. Combining a computer with a digital camera or scanner (see Chapter 8: Photographing Works of Art) allows quick and easy transmission of images worldwide. Images and text can be downloaded and an immediate representation can be available in a matter of seconds or minutes.

Business Cards and Brochures

Other than word of mouth references, your least expensive form of promotion is with the simple business card. The studio and proprietor's name, plus a business logo, address, telephone, e-mail, fax, and Web site are the basic information needed. The background

'CHOSIN POTTERY INC.

4283 Metchosin Road
Victoria, BC Canada V9C 3Z4
(250) 474-2676
www.chosinpottery.ca   chosin@chosinpottery.ca

Our business card background is a photo of the display area of our gallery.

'CHOSIN POTTERY

JUDI DYELLE

Judi Dyelle began pottery in 1962, in Toronto, Ontario. In 1967 she received the Lieutenant Governor's Medal for Excellence and a Canada Council grant to study in Japan with Tatsuzo Shimaoka. She has taught and produced pottery in Toronto, Montreal and Vancouver before moving to Victoria. She has participated in numerous exhibitions. Her work is in many private collections throughout Canada, United States, Japan, Denmark, Iceland, Germany, Australia, China and England.

ROBIN HOPPER

Robin Hopper is one of Canada's finest and best known ceramic artists. He began making pottery in 1956, and has had studios in England, and Eastern Canada before moving to Victoria in 1977. He was the first recipient of the Bronfman Award, Canada's most prestigious annual award in the crafts. He works mainly in porcelain to most benefit the use of coloured glazes developed through considerable ongoing research. The inspiration for his work comes from three main sources; nature, ceramic history and the garden. He is also the author of two books, "The Ceramic Spectrum" and "Functional Pottery". In association with Tara Productions he has produced a wide variety of educational videos. He has lectured throughout Canada, England, the United States, Australia, New Zealand, China and Japan. His work is in many public and private collections worldwide.

THE WORK

We produce a wide range of work, mainly in high-temperature, reduction-fired porcelain. It ranges from one-of-a-kind pieces for decoration or contemplation to an excellent selection of functional pottery for everyday use. This includes mugs, teapots, goblets, pitchers, decanters, bowls, creams and sugars, plates, and a variety of casseroles and serving dishes. All of our functional pottery is oven, microwave and dishwasher proof. The majority of the work is wheel thrown, but we do have a selection of unique handbuilt forms. We also produce special commissions for architectural and interior design use.

The inside of 'Chosin Pottery's three-fold brochure.

Robin Hopper and Judi Dyelle

**4283 Metchosin Rd.
Victoria, B.C., Canada V9C 3Z4**

**TEL/FAX: (250) 474-2676
EMAIL: chosin@chosinpottery.ca
WEB: www.chosinpottery.ca**

OPEN DAILY 10 a.m.–5 p.m.

The front panel of the brochure we use.

to the information can be anything from plain white or colored paper to something that represents the work being done in the particular business. Business cards are often used as the basis of inexpensive printed advertising copy.

A brochure or flyer can be anything from a black and white single sheet to a multiple-fold, full-color graphic document, depending on your budget. It generally includes the same information as the business card, plus whatever additional pictorial or text content is deemed necessary. Usually the simpler the better; in the visual arts, pictures often convey more than words.

Cards and brochures are constantly given away, enclosed with purchases, and mailed to prospective customers. With printed materials, the larger the print run, the cheaper per item the material becomes. I am always amazed at how many I go through, so ordering 10,000 at a time can be fairly economical. The rate of use depends on how many places you can place them—stores, galleries, tourist information centers, hotels, motels, bed and breakfasts, etc., anywhere people pick things up for information, either for immediate use or future reference.

Postcards, Posters, and Catalogs

Photo postcards are a popular and inexpensive way to send images of your work out to a wide audience. Check with different commercial printers, as costs may vary greatly. A number of cards can be printed per sheet and then cut apart, giving a good number for a low price. As with any printing job, the more you order at once, the lower the per-item cost. Another advantage of postcards is the lower rate of postage.

A higher priced alternative to the postcard and brochure is a poster. The quality of photographic images for poster use is critical, so it's advisable to have color transparencies that are at least 4" by 5" for reproduction on a poster. Sometimes a poster is the preferred method of advertising an exhibition. Posters are often done in limited editions and are sent to clients with a history of purchasing works by the featured artist. Even with the added costs of printing and postage, posters are still considerably cheaper than a full catalog and give a big bang for the buck.

Catalogs may be either a printed record of an exhibition, or a publication that is used as a sales tool, documenting your work, its price, and availability. Because a catalog is very expensive to produce, individual artists rarely, if ever, shoulder the cost alone. It is usually a shared cost with the gallery by prior agreement. The most likely way to have your work appear in a catalog is to exhibit at a gallery that produces a catalog as a sales tool. Comparatively few exhibitions have a full catalog until the featured artist is at a high level of credibility, visibility, and acceptance, often referred to as a "blue-chip" artist. Depending on the gallery, public or private, a catalog may or may not be a financially viable possibility. It is, however, an important record of where the artist may be in his work at a given time, and have great relevance in developing important professional credentials. The sales catalog has now been mainly taken over by the personal Web site.

Web Sites and Other Electronic Media
Web Sites

A Web site is the most recent, most effective, and cheapest advertising format to provide instant information on your product to people almost anywhere in the world. The initial development of the site may be costly if you hire a professional to do it, but with some computer skills and a Web site design application, you can do it yourself at home for comparatively little cost. The great benefit of doing your own Web site is that you have full control. As a designer/maker of objects, you are usually the best person to promote yourself. If you don't use a computer, or if you have no faith in your abilities to design a Web site, use the services of a professional designer and work in close contact to develop something that you feel comfortable with and that fully represents you and your work in the most satisfactory way.

A Web site can be quite simple or extremely complex. Make sure that it downloads fast, is easy to navigate, and flows well on any type of computer. It can give a taste of your work, or can become a veritable archive. One artist I know has an image of every object he has ever made on a site that amounts to several hundred pages in length. You need to decide for yourself what the most important purpose of your Web site may be. While many people have been fast to use Web sites to gather information, many artists tell me that, as yet, the sites have been inefficient selling tools. As people generally get more comfortable purchasing over the "net" this may change drastically, although art is best appreciated in its original format and is often "touchy-feely," which doesn't manifest itself on screen. However, as information tools, Web sites are a huge step forward in creating greater understanding and awareness of the visual arts.

CDs

The CD-Rom is an upscale, immediate, electronic portfolio. Extremely compact, it can hold a large number of images or text in various file formats, including small video clips. If you have a CD burner, the cost of producing CDs is very reasonable and can provide a fast and simple way to send your promotional material to galleries, publishers, etc. If you don't have a burner, there are many photo finishers who will put photo images on a CD.

The CD should include your images in a variety of file formats such as jpegs at 72dpi for the Web or general computer viewing, tifs in high resolution (300dpi minimum) for printing and have the capability to be read by both a Mac or PC computer. In this way you have covered all the bases on one disc no matter who you are sending it to. With the use of a digital camera, you can also produce a very inexpensive catalog that is easy to ship.

Videos

Videos can give further information about artists, their production methods, and their finished objects. Three-dimensional visuals of objects in motion capture the qualities of art forms that have height, width, and depth. The opportunity to see a sculpture or other three-dimensional art from all directions almost brings it to life on the flat screen. Detailed close-ups and enlargements can reveal the complexities of the surface, color, and pattern even better than holding the object in your hands and looking at it normally. Formerly expensive to produce, videos can now be made inexpensively with a digital video camera and a computer with suitable video production software. The technology has developed to the point that professional quality videos may be made by the average person untrained in cinematographic technology.

Powerpoint Presentations

Powerpoint is a computer application that uses graphics, text, and slide images to produce a personal presentation. Add sound and music and it makes for a more interesting delivery. It can be output as 35mm slides, overhead transparencies, or even onto paper. It's different from the CD-Rom in that the artist has to be there with his computer to do the presentation. How useful this may be to the average artist is questionable, but it is another possible promotional tool to give greater visibility to the artist and his, or her, works.

With the variety of inexpensive ways for artists to be able to gain exposure for their work, the opportunity for self-promotion and visibility is better now than it ever has been. If you've got something to sell, the ways to let people know about it are wide and varied indeed.

For the most efficient promotion, know yourself, know your product, and know your target market.

Biographical Sketch
Denise Goyer and
Alain Bonneau

Written by Alain Bonneau

Denise Goyer
and Alain Bonneau.

Denise was the first to become involved in ceramics, after studying applied arts (option ceramic) for four years in Montreal, Quebec. In 1970, she persuaded two of her schoolmates to start a studio in a garage that she rented in Saint-Bruno, a Montreal suburb. The adventure lasted two years; one partner left after six months, the other was more interested in teaching and organized classes in the studio. Denise did not really like the idea of teaching, she was more fascinated by learning secrets of the trade and designing new objects. At the time she was developing a line of products (wheel-thrown and slabs) to propose to galleries (retailers). Meanwhile, since 1968 I had been working as a graphic designer. When Denise and her partners split in 1972, I became more present in her studio. After helping and learning for one year, I became convinced that I preferred working in three dimensions. So Denise and I decided we would work together full-time in the near future. In 1973, we designed and built our house and studio in Carignan. It took my father and I one year, part-time, to build it. This house is in the pure French (Bretagne) architectural tradition but designed to answer very specific needs. The back yard is wooded, with a little river, yet we are very close to the city of Montreal.

In January 1975 the team Goyer-Bonneau became a reality. After five years things became clear—Denise was the architect, I was the engineer. In fact, even though Denise had formal ceramic training, our production was collaborative, where creativity and ideas combined with our complicity and ingenuity. She designed a place setting, I designed and made a jigger machine on an electric potter's wheel, using the jiggering process to realize different size plates. Soon, other things became clear—our studio would not be open to

the public. It is a house/studio where the professional life gets mixed with our family life.

Hand throwing was becoming a limitation to our creativity, and we thought slipcasting would be our best option. With the help of ceramic industries such as Sial Inc. and Ceramique de Beauce, Inc. in Quebec, we learned. We learned even more through extensive travel and study at great ceramic centers of Europe including Sévres National Manufacture in Paris, Chastagner Haviland in Limoges, France, Rosenthal China, Zelb and Rosenthal Glass, in Germany, and Wedgwood in England.

Our experience and research in industry gave us an awareness of the technology that we needed and wanted. Now we can spend most of our time (months) creating one object. Then we are able to repeat the idea almost perfectly. The most important thing for us is to convey what is in our mind, our idea, not the amount of effort it took to realize it! For us, a piece does not have to be one-of-a-kind to be unique.

From the outset, we oriented ourselves and our production for the wholesale market. We believed that if there were 20 people selling our production, we would have more opportunities to find those who would like our way of expressing things. When you sell wholesale, you must be willing to work hard. You cannot do it halfway even if you are selling half price. Anyway, it is better than consignment!

Up to eight years ago, we were doing one retail show a year. It was very important for us to know and experience the reaction to our production directly from the retail buyers. Sometimes gallery and store owners or representatives have a tendency to blame the artist if the work does not sell, which is not always true. Selling and marketing the work is a very important part of the process, probably the most expensive one. If you don't sell, you cannot do what you like most, which is to create objects. The money gained by selling finances the materials and time for more making, which in turn allows for more selling. So we learned, after trying nearly everything, that in our trade we must to do it ourselves. Small production is not interesting for agents or representatives; being paid on a percentage basis, volume is important for them. They are not artists, they work for money!

One of the more uncommon experiences we had outside our studio was the industrial production of our designs. A ceramic manufacturer in Canada, Ceramique de Beauce, was under license to produce some of our models: a teapot, cups and saucer, a plate, etc. They had 100 employees, so the volume was there and they were shipping our design all over the planet. We were pleased with the experience and were paid on a royalty basis. It was fair, the ceramic manufacturer was expanding into a new market with innovative designs, and we were being paid without doing the production, thus freeing us for doing more research and giving us financial support to develop new concepts in our studio.

Conclusion

You must believe in what you do if you want people to believe in you. You must have more than one talent, so I suggest forming an association with someone who has complementary talents; it is very important to recognize the talent of your partner. Always remember that behind every great artist there is someone who takes care of the plumbing.

One last thing, you are not just selling your work, you are selling your commitment to your art.

The secret: Be passionate.

Goyer-Bonneau, 2124 Des Tulipes, Carignan, Quebec, Canada J0R 5G2, e-mail: goyer.bonneau@sympatico.ca.

Photo by Jean Longpre.

"*Venus Place Setting.*" Cream porcelain, slipcast. Dinner plate 28 cm, bowl 20 cm, bread plate 15 cm, handleless cup 10 cm high.

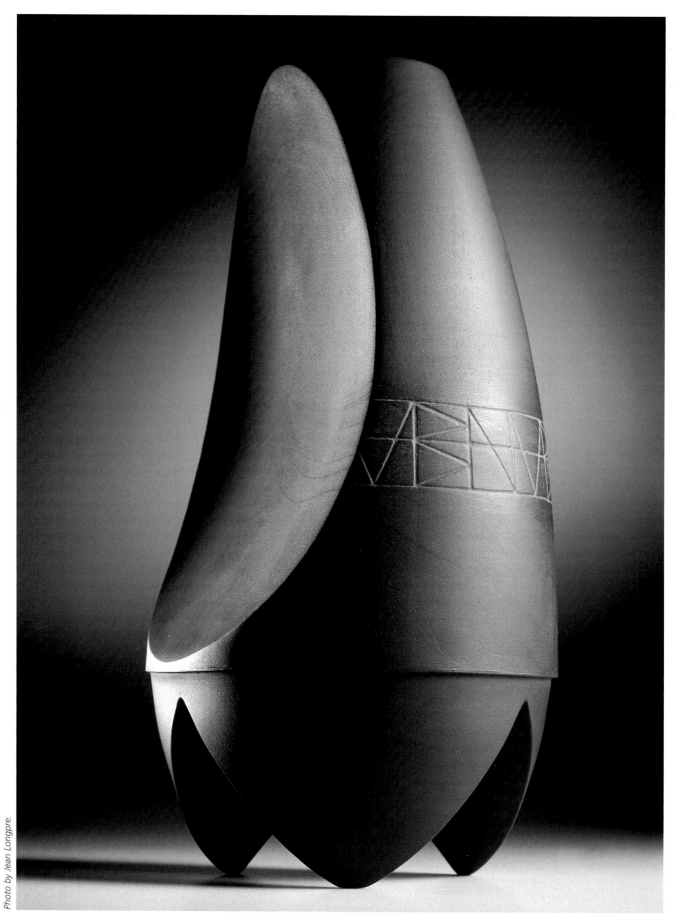

"MBAM Vase." Tripod vase for the Montreal Museum of Fine Arts. Black porcelain, slipcast. 25.5 cm high. 1994.

"The Twins." Vase with lid. Cream porcelain, slipcast. Charles (small) 25 cm tall. Edouard (tall) 35 cm tall. 1999.

Survival Tactics for the Visual Artist   57

"French Curve" and *"un dessous de Venus."* Teapot and handless cup. Black porcelain and cream porcelain, slipcast. Pot 18 cm high x 13.5 cm diameter and cup 10 cm high x 10 cm diameter. *"French Curve"* 1997, *"un dessous de Venus"* 2000.

"Insect." Two service plate; one upside down. Black porcelain, slipcast. 41 cm long x 16 cm. 1999.

Photo by Jean Longpre.

Photo by Jean Longpre.

"Tripod." Fruit bowl. Cream porcelain, slipcast. 11.5 cm high x 21 cm diameter. 1995.

"Black Venus." Black porcelain, slipcast. Dinner plate 28 cm, individual bowl 20 cm.

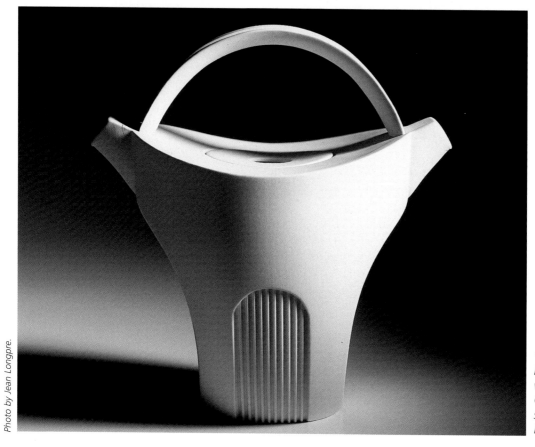

"Entre deux becs." Teapot with two spouts. Cream porcelain, slipcast. 18 cm high x 18 cm.

Biographical Sketch
Patrick Horsley

Patrick Horsley.

Photo by Rick Paulson.

My love of the arts began at an early age. My mother was a great support, along with the encouragement of public school teachers. In a small eastern Washington town with limited resources, no galleries or museums, this was a great help. My first clay experience was in high school. Marriage to my childhood sweetheart followed graduation from high school. After nine days of marriage, I left for two years in the Navy. When I returned, I attended two years of art classes at the local community college, reinforcing the idea of attending an art school.

In 1967, along with my family, I moved to Portland, Oregon, and enrolled in the Museum Art School, a pre-professional institution. My initial interest was in painting but the exposure to people working in clay and the many facets of pottery grabbed my attention. I enjoyed the idea that a person could be self-supporting as an artist.

After four years in art school, studying ceramics, I left. At that time, there were many opportunities for part-time teaching. Teaching enabled me to refine my throwing and forming skills. However, I felt like I was just one or two steps ahead of my students. This gave me a great chance to learn and be paid! At home, I built a small catenary kiln from salvaged bricks. A small back porch served as my first studio. Later I was invited to join a large co-op studio with two other potters, Tom Coleman and Don Sprague. We then built two gas-fired kilns. The experience was good for me because Tom had been making pots for some time and Don was moving from a large group studio into making pots full-time. Working with them and seeing how they used their time, resolved production problems, and came up with new ideas was a joy. This was a great learning expe-

rience for me, which I consider as valuable to me as a university graduate school. Some years later Tom moved to his own studio out in the country. Don and I then moved across town to a rented grocery store. We divided the space in half and shared kiln firings. The pots I made at this time were utilitarian in nature—casseroles, pitchers, mugs, and a lot of bowls and lidded jars. This time sharpened my throwing skills and I gained needed information on clay and glazes.

A few years later I purchased a house with a two-car 24 by 24 foot garage with power, water, and lights. This became my small but well-equipped studio. My clay is custom mixed by my local supplier who I also do research and development for on a part-time basis. I have a part-time studio assistant who works a couple days a week doing various studio jobs. My space is small for the numbers of pots I am trying to make, so everything has its place. At times it gets very crowded until pots are shipped away.

For the last seven years, I have been marketing my decorative work through the American Crafts Council wholesale show in Baltimore, Maryland. At this point, I am taking all the orders that I can fill in a year, then some! We have a studio sale at Christmastime and do our Potters Association Sale in the spring. Other sources of income are commissions from designers, custom direct orders, and invitational shows.

I make 18 different shapes—platters, square plates, and vases of numerous shapes and sizes, with specific weights for each form, from seven-pound vases to 50-pound platters. My glazing is mainly a reverse wax resist technique, with wax patterns that are echoes both of the pot and landscapes of eastern Oregon. I work hard at keeping the work fresh and exciting for myself and my customers. Small drawings of ideas on index cards are stacked all over the studio or pinned to the wall near my wheel so I can look at them over time. I try to introduce three to four new forms each year. In Baltimore, galleries and shops want to see new work. The search for new glazes and colors is an ongoing process. I have just worked for two years to find a new black glaze to replace the oxide saturated glaze I have used for 25 years. Sometimes I feel like I make pots just to fire the kiln and put new glaze tests in.

Inspiration for new ideas comes from many different sources, including design and architecture magazines as opposed to ceramic periodicals. The techniques and tools I make and use make a strong impression on my pottery. The majority of my pots are thrown and altered. Just changing the geometry of thrown shapes gives endless choices to forms. Calling my work "decorative" enables me to charge high prices because they are not limited by their function. I am concentrating on wall platters, plates, and vases, both large and small. Narrowing the choice of forms is very liberating.

Many people have influenced my work, from the architecture of Samuel Mockbee, the ceramics of Ettore Sottsass, to the writing of Paul Theroux, and any kind of travel is always inspiring to me.

If you want to make pottery full-time and make a living, it will take much physical work, endless optimism, and good organization. Marketing, pricing, designing, and working on glaze and clay chemistry also are very important. If you are to stay alive as a potter, you need to remember that you are a small business and not much different from the mechanic down the road.

Patrick Horsley, 6401 S.E. Raymond, Portland, OR 97206, e-mail: horsley@teleport.com.

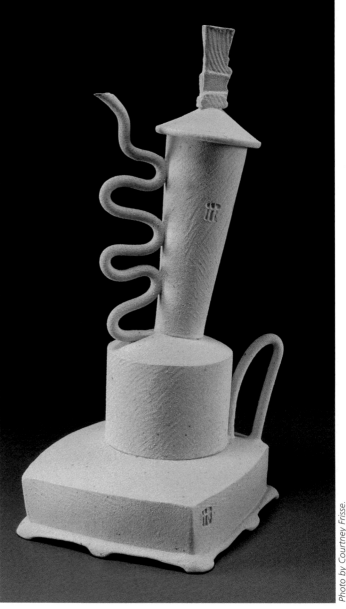

Photo by Courtney Frisse.

Teapot. Thrown and altered stoneware. Matt yellow ash glaze. 16" x 5" x 5".

Basket shape. Thrown and altered stoneware. Slip with wax pattern. 22" x 6" x 10".

Platter. Bronze, cone 6 reduction. Oxide saturated glaze.

Group of vases and platters. Cone 6 reduction. Various sizes and glazes.

Biographical Sketch
Pauline Pelletier

Pauline Pelletier.

Photo by Pierre Fortin.

My decision to become a potter certainly wasn't a preconceived one. Toward the end of the 1960s, I was invited to attend an event held in Quebec City, where pottery was being unloaded from a gas kiln. I immediately fell in love with what I saw, incredulous that such an experience would excite me so much. That evening I discovered the possibility of expressing myself in a way that would enable me to transform matter by giving it meaning and a new purpose. Totally fascinated, I knew that I would become a potter. A long period of apprenticeship followed, during which time I discovered the pleasures of making useful objects that are beautiful and yet communicate with the potential user of the object. I read and reread the books of Daniel Rhodes and Bernard Leach with passionate intensity.

I quickly became interested in porcelain and in casting techniques. This radiant clay had all sorts of new possibilities for design and decoration. After interminable hours of firing in a huge catenary kiln, my very first tenmokus, kakis, celadons, and copper red wares were drawn from the kiln. I packed the car with boxes of pottery and was off to all sorts of boutiques or exhibits.

My first teacher was of Swiss origin and influenced me greatly. I attended a number of pottery workshops held in the United States, Japan, and the rest of Canada. I felt isolated here in Quebec City and wanted to see everything so I could learn everything. From very early on I was fascinated by pottery from Asia.

Of course there were some setbacks in those early days—batches that didn't quite turn out, temporarily shattered hopes—but such disappointments were gradually erased with time, and I have mostly fond recollec-tions of this period, with the exception of when fire ravaged part of my workshop in the winter of 1976. My studio and kiln were severely damaged from the fire and spent six months entombed in ice. I had no choice but to rebuild the kiln and warehouse. I needed money, so I calculated my needs and set out to produce 1,000 flowerpots to fund the reconstruction process.

It is hard for those who have never done it to imagine all the energy that the operation of a working pottery studio requires. You have to approach prospective clients politely and learn to accept indifference, rejection, and those all too frequent days without sales, and in spite of it all, you must never lose faith in your product or question your primary objective.

With time, it became obvious that I needed to find agents to handle the wholesale marketing of my products over the entire country and thus ensure production stability. This decision enabled me to devote my time, in the early 1980s, to opening a gallery/boutique in old Quebec City's tourist neighborhood. The boutique served both as a sales outlet for my own wares and as a way to raise the profile and market the works of a number of other artisans. Above and beyond working at the boutique and with my representatives, I always made sure that once or twice a year I would participate in a craft fair or prepare an exhibit (alone or in a group) showing new works. Working with an assistant, I discovered all the energy as well as the enriching experience provided by teamwork. In our individually focused profession, the important role of apprentices and collaborators is, unfortunately, too often ignored.

I was the mother of six young children at the time and I could devote myself completely to my new passion only after my offspring were in bed. Escaping to my workshop in the basement and toiling nightly, unaware of time passing, I often labored tirelessly very late into the night. It became obvious that I would have to organize my time in a more rational manner. Thanks to the moral support of a very understanding and patient husband, as well as to a bank loan granted by a rather distrustful bank manager, I bought an old house that, with the help of my friends, I transformed first into a school/workshop and then into a true potter's workshop. It goes without saying that these new mortgage obligations forced me to produce. I had only one choice—to work, and to keep on working, in spite of the challenges of simultaneously learning the trade, with prejudices of all sorts (directed toward a married woman with children still at home), and inevitable periods of despondency.

I started to develop a team studio to ensure continuity of production. Without it, I would never have been able to leave the workshop for several months in 1986 to pursue a professional development internship at the Manufacture Nationale in Sèvres, France, or make various trips to Asia and elsewhere. This allowed participation in a number of personally stimulating exhibits that were also beneficial for my workshop.

Without my team, I would sometimes have had problems going as far as I did in developing various techniques or in fine-tuning manufacturing procedures. It would be unthinkable for me to sum up my career without acknowledging the importance of those who stayed by my side during all those years.

To anyone attracted by pottery and wishing to make it a vocation: Make sure you are able to regularly devote many long hours to your craft. In other words, the reality is a bit different from the clichéd idyllic image of pottery conveyed at training workshops. One thing is for sure: Your earnings are not always commensurate with the number of hours you work. Being a potter means being able to do work that touches on all sorts of related areas, not only artistic, manual, and technical, but also with regards to communications and commerce. A potter must be equipped to deal with all elements of the trade.

After all these years of work that have enabled me to earn a living as a member of the world's most wonderful profession, I must say that pottery still fascinates me as much as when I started. My only regret is not having begun my life's work 20 years earlier!

Pauline Pelletier, 1382 Rue Provancher, Cap Rouge, Quebec, Canada G1Y 3C6.

Photo by Pierre Fortin.

Set of Three. Thrown porcelain, reduction fired to cone 11. Copper red glaze and metallic gold luster. 2002.

Vessel. Thrown porcelain, saggar fired to cone 04. Decorated with sulfate and chloride. 22 karat gold leaves. 1999.

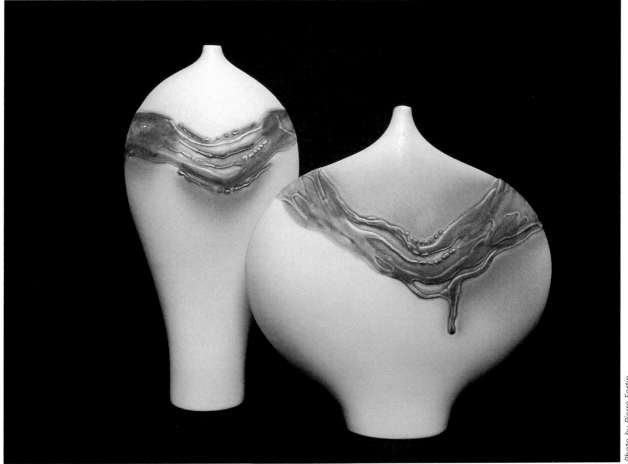

Two Vases. Porcelain slipcast, reduction fired to cone 11. White matt glaze, strip of fabric added for decoration. 1988.

Hippo Bowl. Slipcast porcelain, reduction fired to cone 11. Top is metallic gold luster, hippos electroplated copper. 1993.

Chapter 5

Legal Considerations

By E.M. (Yeti) Agnew, Arts Lawyer

Laws are what make civilization civil. They form the code of conduct and ethics basic to democratic society. Without laws, anarchy might prevail. Law comes from various sources. There is *statute law*—the law that federal governments and legislatures write. Statutes or acts can provide a framework for dealings. The American *Uniform Commercial Code* and the various Canadian provincial *Sales of Goods Acts* are examples of statutes that govern commercial relationships.

There is *common law*—the decisions written by judges in rulings on individual cases. Sometimes judges will listen to evidence about "custom of the trade" and make findings regarding the unofficial practices that are accepted as the unwritten rules of particular businesses. The decisions and rulings are, in the course of time, digested in legal texts by lawyers and law professors seeking to find patterns in legal decisions. Sometimes statutes and acts codify or amend these judge-made rules.

Finally, there are the rules in contracts that people make between themselves to govern their own conduct. Contracts can have provisions that override legislation as long as they are legal, and contracts can contradict what would be the expected response of a judge. Contracts are most frequently used as a ready reference as to the terms of a transaction without the need to have an extensive knowledge of legislation and common law.

If you are not certain of the law affecting a business transaction, the safest course is to have a written contract.

What Is a Contract?

A contract is an agreement between two or more persons for the exchange of property (including money) or promises of future performance. Contracts can be verbal or written. Contracts can be part of an invoice, a purchase order, a letter, a proposal, or they can be drafted as separate documents.

Contracts are the foundation on which business is conducted. Contracts establish the legal rights and obligations of the parties to the contract. The best contract is one that is easily understood and covers the concerns of the parties and addresses the possibilities

that may occur in a given situation. Written contracts are preferred because their provisions are readily ascertainable.

Why You Should Use Written Contracts

Verbal contracts are risky because memories or understandings of a transaction frequently differ. Some verbal contracts are unenforceable because legislators, aware of the problems of verbal contracts, have stipulated that verbal contracts that cannot be performed within a specified time or that involve more than a specified amount of money or a certain type of property are not enforceable. An exception may arise if one or more parties have partially performed their responsibilities under the contract. However, even if an exception applies, proving that a particular understanding of a verbal contract is the correct version can be difficult.

A carefully drafted written contract sets out the entire deal with a customer or supplier. This prevents their trying to unilaterally change arrangements at a later date and causing you expense. Properly drafted contracts help avoid unnecessary and costly disputes.

Battle of the Forms

For convenience, many businesses prepare standard contracts to use with all their customers or suppliers. They then tailor these standard forms to specific jobs by filling in blank spaces or providing attachments that set out the exact services to be performed, the products to be furnished, the time for performance, the cost, and any circumstances that would excuse complete and prompt performance.

Consequently, businesses sometimes exchange purchase orders and invoices that contain conflicting terms. Resolving these conflicts can be extremely costly. Generally, courts compare all the forms: they ignore all the conflicting terms and apply all the terms that do not conflict. This can result in a deal quite different from the one you intended! You should promptly read all the fine print on the contracts, invoices, and purchase orders you receive from customers and suppliers. Whenever these contain provisions that you do not like or that conflict with your forms, discuss the conflicts with the other side as soon as possible. This helps everyone avoid expense and adverse results that can otherwise arise.

Some Key Contract Provisions

The terms of the contract—the who, what, where, when, and how of the agreement—define the binding promises of each party to the contract. Make an outline of these items for your contract. Another list, setting out the hopes, fears, goals, and risks that surround the transaction will lead to the additional provisions to better protect your interests.

Write in ordinary English. Write in short sentences. Use the active tense to use words more efficiently and make their meaning more clear. Use the same word whenever you mean the same thing (repetitive language is preferred in contract writing). Be careful and aware when using words such as "may," "must," "should," "will," and "shall." Do not rely solely on rules of grammar to differentiate between the future tense and the imperative voice of a verb. Not everyone follows the same rules.

Organize the various provisions—it helps identify missing provisions. A written contract should include all the necessary provisions. Here are some suggestions:

1. Identify it as a "Contract" and put in a date in the first lines. It makes it easy to describe the contract in other documents in a precise way, such as the "December 20, 2002, Contract for Consulting Services."

2. Who? Parties: Your contract should correctly state the full name of each person involved in the contract. For example, if you and your client have incorporated your businesses, the contract should state the full legal names of the corporations. The agreement will be more user-friendly if you insert full contact information for the people you are dealing with, including their titles, phone and fax numbers, and e-mail addresses.

3. Who else? Guarantors: In cases where you deal with a person who has already incorporated their businesses and you contract with their corporation, only the corporation is responsible for performing under the contract. If you also want them to be personally responsible, you name them and indicate that fact in the contract. They then sign the contract on behalf of their corporation and for themselves personally.

4. Why? Background or recitals: Sometimes a brief explanation of why the parties are contracting can usefully set the stage. Be careful not to include boasts that may be interpreted as warranties.

5. What? Make sure your contract fully and completely states all the obligations of each party to the contract, including all deadlines for delivery and payment.

Consider requesting progress payments and specifying time periods for necessary approvals. If your contract refers to other writings, attach copies of those writings to the contract as exhibits or schedules. Have someone who is not familiar with the transaction read the contract and tell you what the contract says. Can your reader describe what you expect to happen under the contract, with the appropriate details of who, what, when, where, and how?

6. How? Answering this question often adds very valuable detail to the contract. Should more be written into the contract?

7. Express warranties: These days, to successfully compete, businesspeople often explicitly guarantee that their products and services will meet certain specifications. In legal jargon these are called express warranties. If you offer an express warranty, your contract should describe it and state that you offer no express warranties besides those stated. If express warranties are not part of your deal with your customer, your written contract should say that. Then your customer cannot claim that you failed to honor an express warranty.

8. Implied warranties: Even if you do not offer an express warranty, you may still be required to stand behind your products because the law may impose implied warranties. Two types of implied warranties frequently cause concern. The first type is the implied warranty of fitness for a particular purpose. It exists when you know that your customer has a particular need and is relying on your advice to select appropriately. If this implied warranty is not part of your deal with your customer, have your contract say so. The second type of implied warranty is the implied warranty of merchantability. It exists in every sale of a product. It requires your product to be reasonably satisfactory to the typical customer. If this implied warranty is not part of your deal, your contract should state that. Ask yourself if your customer is typical.

9. Copyright: Use explicit language to deal with copyright ownership, assignments of copyright, and licensing of copyright. Be aware that national laws can differ substantially on the subject of copyright, particularly on the ownership of copyright in work ordered from third parties. Court decisions in this area also vary from place to place based on their various understandings of the customs of the trade. Specifically address the subject of copyright ownership to avoid future disputes. Copyright ownership is an economic right. There are other economic rights such as the *droit de suite* (resale royalty right), which should also be included in a contract to assure the right to assert such a right in the future.

10. Moral rights: Moral rights are also dealt with very differently under American and Canadian copyright legislation and under contract and property law in various state and provincial jurisdictions. Accordingly, creators should be very specific in detailing their rights to maintain the integrity of work, the right to make modifications to the work and its siting, the right to be associated with the work as its creator, the future use of the work, etc.

11. When? The term or duration of the contract and the timelines to be observed are important. "Time is of the essence" means that not meeting a deadline breaches the contract.

12. Why not? Excuses for performance: A provision known as a *force majeure* (irresistible force, act of God, etc.) clause excuses performance due to events beyond a person's control, such as strikes, natural disasters, riots, etc. For example, if you will be unable to complete a job without information from your customer, your contract should excuse your delay for that reason. Consider adding a provision that allows you to terminate the contract if conditions that excuse performance persist for longer than a specified time.

13. What if? Remedies for breach of contract: If you are accused of breaching (failing to fully and timely perform) your contract, proving whether and how much you should pay can be extremely expensive and time-consuming. Therefore, your contracts should specify the maximum amount you will have to pay in case of a breach and how long your customers have to notify you of a problem. Be aware that a judge may ignore unreasonable specifications.

14. Damages for unexcused failure to perform: What happens if either party's failure to perform is unexcused? Your contract should specify the types of damages that will accrue, so that each side will know them in advance. For example, damages for nonperformance can include the cost of goods purchased or delivered and lost profits. The exact amount of damages (*liquidated damages*) can be specified in advance when, under the circumstances, proof of actual losses may be difficult. Also, your contract must expressly provide for interest and lawyer's fees if you want to recover those items.

15. Interest and lawyer's fees: Even in an era of low interest rates, most businesses cannot afford to finance their customers. If you want to charge interest on unpaid bills, your contract must state what the interest rate is and when interest charges begin to accrue. If you want to charge your customers for lawyer's fees incurred to collect unpaid bills, your contract must state that you intend to do that.

Otherwise, you probably will not be able to recover interest or lawyer's fees, even if your customer unjustifiably withholds payment.

16. Where? Choice of law and jurisdiction: Many businesses have transactions with someone who is not physically located in the same state or province or who does not transact significant amounts of business with others in that state or province. As noted previously, crossing material borders is also becoming more common. In these circumstances, a contract should specify whose statutes and judge-made laws will govern the deal (such as the law of the state of New York) and the location at which the parties must appear to resolve disputes (such as the courts in Toledo). Otherwise, you may be forced to litigate in a distant forum under unfamiliar laws.

17. Consider mediation: Litigation is very expensive. There are alternatives available that may be more attractive. Increasing numbers of businesses are turning to mediation and/or arbitration. People's understanding of what is involved in mediation or arbitration can differ widely, so a clause with detailed specifics of how the process will be conducted is necessary. Arbitration/mediation can be an expeditious, inexpensive way to resolve disputes. Unlike litigation, arbitration/mediation does not necessarily require the assistance of a lawyer, and the procedural rules can be relatively simple. If you have a complicated deal, arbitration may not be a good alternative because the process may be too streamlined.

Business Organization Contracts

In business, having appropriate written contracts is the "ounce of prevention" that is "worth a pound of cure." This is particularly true when entering into longer term business relationships with others. Unfortunately, these relationships are too often the ones most neglected in terms of contract documentation.

Start by knowing how your relationships can be characterized in law and what consequences flow from the different characterizations. Danger can lurk in undocumented sharing of space and equipment, or poorly papered relationships with persons who obtain business leads. Have a proper lease. Have a property sharing agreement. Appoint an agent (or dealer) for selected purposes only, or for all purposes. Or enter into an appropriate and proper partnership agreement.

Legislatures have passed statutes governing partnerships. Unfortunately, the various statutes provide unsatisfactory agreements for most partnerships. Shareholder relationships in small corporations are governed by much of the same corporate law that governs publicly traded multinationals in the absence of shareholder agreements. Partnership agreements and shareholder agreements are needed when people are joined together in a common business enterprise.

Partnership and shareholder agreements are very similar in many respects and should address the three Ds: *death, disability*, and *disagreement*. What happens if a partner or shareholder dies? Will the estate become a participant in the business? If not, how will the estate be bought out? What happens if a partner or shareholder becomes disabled? How long can they stay in the business without being able to work in it? How will a purchase be financed? What happens if the parties disagree in the future? Is there a "shotgun" provision under which one party offers to buy out the other party and by making the offer indicates the fairness of the proposal by offering to sell their stake on the same terms? Or is a shotgun provision unfair because of the different financial resources of the parties and so another mechanism should be used?

Consult a lawyer to make sure your contract is properly drafted and contains all the necessary provisions. Written contracts will save you time and money.

Conclusion

Anything that hinders delivery of your best work detracts from your bottom line. Disputes with customers are perhaps the worst hindrances. Using properly prepared written contracts can protect you from customer disputes and help make your business successful.

E.M. (Yeti) Agnew, Agnew, Gladstone LLP, 215 Carlton St., Toronto, Ontario, Canada M5A 2K9.

Will Ruggles (back) and
Douglass Rankin (front).

Photo by Linda Harkley.

We moved to the isolated community of Buladean, in the mountains of western North Carolina, in the spring of 1980. Leaving the flat countryside of Wisconsin, we found these rich mountains that have nourished us, and Rock Creek Pottery, for the past 22 years.

Our paths in clay became clear in 1975 when, in different places, we both took workshops with Warren MacKenzie. Watching the clay move effortlessly under his fingers and form itself into cups, bowls, and teapots marked not only by his personality, but by centuries of pottery ancestors, somehow made pots real for us. We first met in 1976 while apprenticing with Randy Johnston in River Falls, Wisconsin. Randy's enthusiasm for pots, stoked by his recent experience of working with Tatsuzo Shimaoka in Mashiko, Japan, was brilliant fuel for our own passion. Working free, in exchange for education, we fully immersed ourselves in the fundamentals of being potters. In 1980 we began Rock Creek Pottery.

Loving the light salt and wood firing—the process and finished qualities—we built a three-chamber wood-fired noborigama kiln. Conserving fuel and human energy for making reasonably priced daily ware was Will's design objective. Abundant waste wood from local sawmills provided fuel. We built a shed frame over the kiln and roofed it with canvas. For clay we emulated our pottery ancestors, mixing slip with a cement hoe in a stock-watering tank. Building wooden framed drying racks with sheep fence bottoms, we put down cotton sheets and poured in buckets of clay mixed to cake-batter consistency. These, stacked up and topped off with tin roofs, allowed a ton of clay to air dry in two to three weeks. There was a horse barn on the land and the owners (we were care-taking their sheep farm) gave us permission to use it for our workshop. Building ware racks and benches for our wheels, we were making pots by summertime, and by spring of the following year we were accepted into the Washington and Philadelphia Craft Shows.

These provided our foundation for marketing. Not only were both excellent retail venues, especially for the few utilitarian potters allowed in, but galleries used them to recruit people for wholesale work. Within a year and a half we had a good start on supporting ourselves, and for many years our sales pattern remained much the same, with about half the pots sold retail and half wholesale. We made lots of pots, firing our kiln six times a year. To avoid wholesale shows, we maintained contact with the shops owners, typically keeping galleries three to ten years. We made delivery runs to six to ten shops at a time, taking the occasional pot back that hadn't sold, and the delivery fees funded vacations with city friends. Also a surprising number of folks visited the Pottery, including pottery classes on field trips from nearby Penland School.

Three years into our care-taking job we realized we needed a real kiln shed. Almost every time we fired, it rained. And though the owners would reimburse us for improvements on the place if we left, the time and energy needed to build a pottery would have to be spent again. We needed to invest ourselves in our own place, and luckily by then the owners were willing to sell, introducing us to our first real expense.

A dozen years passed when suddenly we realized that pottery days were too long, and there were too many of them in a row. We cut back one kiln a year, raised our prices, and in mid-October of 1995 we began our annual Home Sale, during the peak weekend of fall color. Nine leaf seasons have passed since that first sale, and with them many things have changed.

In 1996, while riding in a car, Will was rear-ended by a tractor and trailer. Soft tissue damage that still limits his abilities six years later necessitated considerable adjustment to life at Rock Creek Pottery. Our electricity comes from a micro-hydro generating system that we set up after three years here without power. But to avoid our penchant for the "night shift," we had never wired the Pottery. In order to continue making pots, Will had to begin throwing standing up at an electric wheel, though he still cuts feet on our low momentum Korean-style kick wheels. Most wedging was taken over by a pugmill, and gradually we have been investing in nine-pound, quarter-inch kiln shelves.

Mixing clay by the slip method still seems to be the most efficient way to make a lively clay body, but our hoe has been replaced by a drill with a sheetrock putty bit, and we move slip from the tank to the racks with a sump pump. Our clay body includes iron-rich clay from behind our kiln and crude kaolin from a local mica operation. These native materials enliven the clay. Making 1,500 pounds of clay takes about four hours, from dry materials to throwing clay, stowed in our storage box. Comparing the price of premixed clay, this is still the best money we make potting.

We teach a couple of workshops a year, and several of these have been in building wood kilns with designs derived from our Rock Creek climbing kiln. These are state-of-the-art constructions built for educational facilities, but still our old beast plugs along. The main firebox has been rebuilt, and a couple of years ago, in a hair-raising renovation project, we jacked up the catenary arch of the first chamber and replaced the fire-face wall and flues.

Our income from pots has changed from intense wholesaling and craft fairs. Now most of our sales are made from the showroom in our barn. Since Will's injury, we make fewer pots, but not sharing the income with shops has made up for our production decrease. We also participate in numerous gallery shows, largely to hold up the flag for utilitarian pots.

Computers entered our lives after our first Home Sale. After Douglass hand addressed 600 sale announcements designed on a word processor, the need for a database and layout program became obvious. As time passes we use the computer more and more. In recent years design work has expanded since Will finds computer work a great deal less painful than throwing. He consults with potters interested in building wood kilns, often designs their kilns, and sometimes builds them. He also does graphics and Web site design for ourselves and others. This work is a nice complement to the pottery.

Our story, as we write it, has been blessed with extreme good fortune. This we acknowledge and honor. But hopefully we can distill some fundamental principles that have made it possible.

Education is essential. Before setting up our business here we had spent eight years each being obsessed by clay and pots. There was formal study through college, workshops, travel, and apprenticing, but also endless evenings feasting on books and handling old pots at every opportunity. Once on a long trip with Willem Gebben we took turns reading Bernard Leach's *Beyond East and West* out loud as the car sailed down the road. By the time we set up, we had a wide knowledge of utilitarian pots from many cultures, and enough technical skills to begin our own interpretations. Many young potters are defeated by beginning to produce pots to sell before they really understand what pots they have in their hearts.

Get help from any and all available sources—family, spouse, grants, apprenticeships, and residencies. Our apprenticeships were vital training for us, and Douglass' work with Randy was partially supported by a National Endowment for the Arts Apprenticeship grant. At Hillcrest Pottery, where we built our first wood kiln, worked out our clay-making system, and figured out leather-hard slipping and glazing, the rent for three of us was $60 a month. After moving here we lived rent-free for our first three years, and when we began to purchase our property, we had support from our families.

We practice the economy of thrift. Doing what we can for ourselves can save a lot, since our pottery time is often worth less than say, carpenters or electricians. Our cycles of throwing, firing, and marketing have always integrated intervals for construction and maintenance, helping to keep our overhead low. Our kiln was made with inexpensive materials, many of which were salvaged, and unlike the deluxe models we have built in schools, ours has a sand floor. When we started shooting our own slides, the equipment was paid for with the cost of two professional photo sessions.

Learning how *not* to spend money is an art form most working potteries practice. But sometimes saving money can bite back. Lots of truckers operate in our county and while constructing our kiln and first gathering clay ingredients, we used back hauls to get large quantities of inexpensive materials. It took us a year to ascertain that a clay body problem was from the remaining five tons of a 10-ton batch of fireclay stock-

Three soup bowls. Wheel thrown with cut feet. White stoneware with kaolin slips, metal slip and glaze decoration. Wood fired, cone 9-10 with salt and soda. 3½" high x 6½" diameter.

piled in our barn. Also, saving by buying inferior quality tools is false thrift. The Stihl chain saw we purchased 22 years ago still runs great after cutting countless cords of wood.

Two working together is distinctly more efficient than potting alone, perhaps doubling output without substantially increasing the overhead. This points to the efficacy of sharing workspace and tools where possible.

Pricing pots is one of the most difficult arenas we have faced, but one that must be relentlessly confronted. The utilitarian pot is completed in use, so we need prices to be low enough to encourage that, while still providing us lifestyle support. We sometimes agonize over raising the price of a mug one dollar, but there are few $60 farmhouses to rent nowadays.

Selling pots involves enabling people to "own" them. At craft fairs we notice shoppers expressing obvious affection toward something, yet this is sometimes mixed with confusion about what it is they are attracted to. Often, after just explaining how the fire has flashed the surface and deposited ash on a handle, the light dawns in their faces and knowledge gives them permission to make connection. Also, people like to come to our place and see how and where the pots are made. Leaving, they take home something beautiful to use, but also they take a piece of a world that nurtures them.

The tools we use for educating people about our pots include articles we write, our craft fair booth, cards, sale announcements, and our Web site. These all represent us and our work and great effort goes into creating them with standards equal to the pots.

To make it all possible, good health remains a focus. When Will was hurt, our back dependency for every phase of our business and lifestyle hit us like that semi. Every aspect of potting—hauling kiln wood and firewood for house and pottery, maintenance, even household sweeping—was impaired or impossible. During the first year after the accident, Douglass injured her back picking up jobs normally divided between two people. For health we meditate, practice Tai Chi, do back and aerobic exercise, get bodywork, and grow an organic garden that feeds us seven months of the year. And in the pottery, we systematically implement ways to reduce stress.

Making pots is not usually a lucrative or easy occupation. A career in pots should only come from need, when this expression is necessary to live. Pots made from the heart can honestly communicate to another heart. But if what we say does not touch others enough to support us, in "potting for love," at least we are nurtured by the quest for beauty. The pressure of needing money can squeeze this path of beauty into an uncomfortable corner. But if we "have to do it," a way will be found.

Rock Creek Pottery, 1971 Huges Gap Rd., Bakersville, NC 28705, e-mail: rcp@m-y.net, Web site: www.rockcreekpottery.com.

Photo by Will Ruggles.

Hexagonal covered jar. Wheel thrown and altered while on the wheel. Alteration of body and lid articulated at soft leather-hard. White stoneware with kaolin slips, metal slip, and glaze decoration. Wood fired, cone 9-10 with salt and soda. 12" high.

Cane handle teapot. White stoneware with kaolin slip, metal slip and glaze decoration. Wood fired, cone 9-10 with salt and soda. 9" high.

"Moroccan" jar. Wheel thrown. White stoneware with kaolin slip, metal slip, and glaze decoration. Wood fired, cone 9-10 with salt and soda. 11" high.

Rectangular bottle. Wheel thrown and altered while on the wheel. Shoulder and neck added at leather-hard. White stoneware with kaolin slip, metal slip, and glaze decoration. Wood fired, cone 9-10 with salt and soda. 12" high.

Paddled bottle. Wheel thrown and squeezed on the wheel. Further altered at wettest stage possible. Coil feet added at soft leather-hard. White stoneware with kaolin slip, metal slip, and glaze decoration. Wood fired, cone 9-10 with salt and soda. 7" high.

Photo by Will Ruggles.

Photo by Will Ruggles.

Square box. Wheel thrown and squared while on the wheel. Squaring articulated and coil feet added at soft leather-hard. White stoneware with kaolin slips, metal slip, and glaze decoration. Wood fired, cone 9-10 with salt and soda. 7" high.

Three-quart pitcher. White stoneware with kaolin slip, metal slip, and glaze decorations. Wood fired, cone 9-10 with salt and soda. 12" high.

Biographical Sketch
Laurie Rolland

Laurie Rolland.

Photo by Larry Westlake.

My father was a woodworker whose many interests and abilities provided fertile ground for development in my youth. He modeled the lifestyle of a maker that I would eventually choose. His romantic yet practical attitude toward life influences me still. I experimented with various mediums, and ultimately found that clay best suited my as yet unrecognized but burgeoning compulsion to "make things."

After several years in western Canada, I moved back to Ontario and took an intensive clay course at a college in Toronto. Four women potters exerted a critical influence at this time. Judy Lowry was one of my instructors there; I much admired her work and with her advice and encouragement decided to learn my trade more fully and enroll full-time at Sheridan College School of Crafts and Design, as until then I was basically self-taught. The projects that Angela Fina, my second year master, gave us triggered a love of assembly of multiple parts that still remains strong. Angela's decision to leave a secure and lucrative teaching post to return to potting was and is an inspiration to me. Christine Dell, another Sheridan graduate, was exhibiting sensitive, colorful, hand-built, and non-functional ceramics. She was successful and she was from my hometown of Orillia. I could do it too! My goal was to make my living as a potter, as it is the making that inspires and motivates me. A small book on the life and work of Clarice Cliff confirmed this idea as possible. The examples of these successful potters was critical, because they were women continuing a tradition that in contemporary Western culture was dominated by men. The influence of the 1960s encouraged the idea of independent work as an integrated lifestyle.

The year before I graduated in 1978, I set up a studio in the alley behind the major Toronto street that we lived on. The apartment was a third floor walkup above a hairdressing salon. The empty building behind the adjacent shoe repair proved adequate for my pottery; with space upstairs for another to share expenses. From the beginning I was planning for what was practical and do-able, working toward realistic and achievable goals. Everything was secondhand, salvaged, or handmade. Shelves, dollies, pallets, gas heater, and a huge scale were scavenged from a defunct candy store. The $30 kiln (shoehorned out of a Rosedale mansion) helped to eventually purchase a larger, newer one. Using second-hand equipment is an excellent way to get started. I spent my final year at Sheridan developing work that I would be able to produce in that studio. As the situation did not allow large wood, gas, or salt kilns, I focused on developing a vocabulary that enhanced electric kiln firing. Many of my building techniques and surface treatments have resulted from this conscious decision to take advantage of oxidation firing. Hand-built and structurally decorated with colored clays, slips, and stains, this early work was based on the functional format.

The artificial limiting of choices can be extremely helpful in defining a focus and direction. Staying within the confines of oxidation firing and learning how best to work with it has become, after 30 years of work and development, the best way for me to realize my ideas. It is no longer a restriction but a direction. The circumstances requiring a small operation when first beginning are no longer the same, although I choose to remain so. Working solo, without distractions, suits the regular nine-to-five work hours I keep and the radio dial stays where I want it. Remaining small means I am entirely independent, free from large overheads, employee concerns, etc. and free to take risks with new ideas. I work for most of the year producing a limited line of hand-built, functionally based "repeat" work, then take several months solely to develop new work for exhibition. The skills developed doing the repeat work inform these new ideas. This time is extremely important to maintain a central core of ideas and fulfillment.

I sell a limited amount of work wholesale, do one quality retail show a year, and sell the rest on consignment. This allows all of my work to change and grow as I decide. I encourage marks that are a result of process. The forms and surfaces of ancient ceramics and especially of ritual objects provide not only inspiration for my work but underline how the marks of those early makers connect me with the song of the universe. The individual "pushing 'good enough' into something better" using universal symbols in a language that is clay unites us through time and space. There is also an organic intent that is evident in all of my work, for I am surrounded by what inspires me—the ocean, our gar-

den, the forest. Being a potter and part of such a noble profession is important to my identity as a maker, for it helps to place my work in a context of meaning. The traditions of the functional and the ritual object are the poles around which my work revolves.

In 1999, 10 years after returning to British Columbia, my new partner and I built a shared pottery studio/woodworking shop ourselves. My second floor space was designed to specifically suit my working methods. Windows were carefully placed to prevent glare. I work standing up so the correct height of 38" on my custom table was very important. My kilns are in a small, separately vented room. The old candy shelves from the first Toronto studio are still used to hold glaze materials. There is a tremendous satisfaction for me in the process itself. For some potters, keeping going is often harder than getting started. By taking risks and letting go of what is certain, it is possible to stay passionate and engaged for 30 years! An attitude of exploration and change is what has kept me inspired, motivated, and satisfied with being a potter.

Laurie Rolland, Westly Site, C25, RR#1, Sechelt, British Columbia, Canada V0N 3A0.

Photo by Laurie Rolland.

"Circinate." Hand-built, cone 6 oxidation. 51 cm long x 15 cm high x 34 cm deep. 2002.

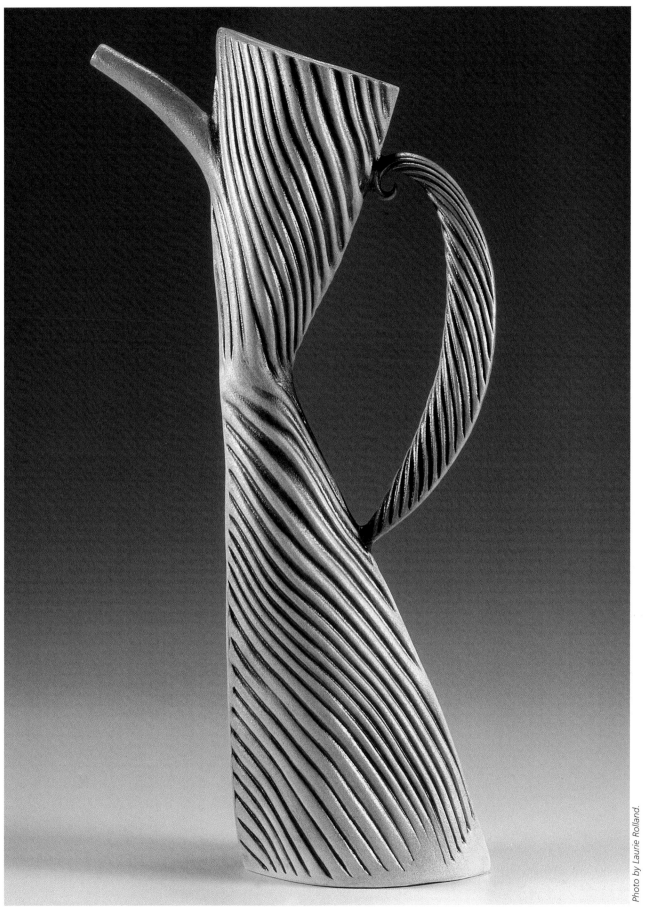

Jug. Hand-built, cone 6 oxidation. 46 cm high. 2002.

Photo by Laurie Rolland.

Teapot. Thrown and hand-built, cone 6 oxidation. 33 cm high. 2002

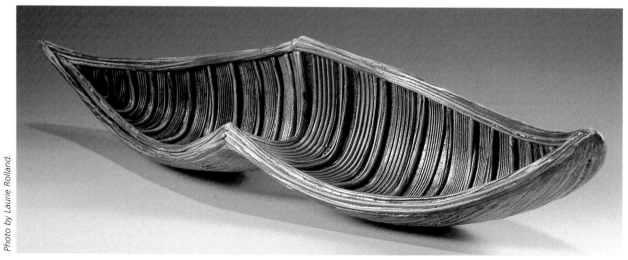

"Mitosis Series #2." Hand-built, cone 6 oxidation. 73 cm long x 1 cm high x 1 cm deep. 2002.

Biographical Sketch
Pam Birdsall
and Tim Worthington

Pam Birdsall and Tim Worthington.

Photo by Mary Dixon.

We, Pam Birdsall and Tim Worthington, opened the doors of Birdsall-Worthington Pottery Ltd. on a sunny July day in 1977 in the picturesque town of Mahone Bay. This small coastal town, known for its famous three churches, is a popular tourist location on Nova Scotia's South Shore. We have become well known for our distinctive slip-decorated pottery, classic forms with delicately feathered slip decoration, and custom-made commemorative plates.

Pam's clay career began as a surprise to her in 1970. She was attending the Nova Scotia College of Art and Design, wanting to focus on apparel design to develop her interest in clothing and intricate needlework. During the Foundation Year Program, she fell in love with clay, its history, and the role pots play in daily life. Working with clay satisfied her attention to detail blended with the practicality of form and function.

While at NSCAD, Walter Ostrom and Homer Lord were our main influences, peppered with many internationally known ceramic artists. One of these visitors was Robin Hopper, who demonstrated slip decoration, which in hindsight can be seen as a "career focusing moment" for Pam.

"I was enthralled with every aspect of Robin's demo. Applying one wet clay over another, then moving a sharp needle through them, blending and creating such flowing designs, was pure magic. I've developed my own style of drawing with slips over the last 25 years and I still enjoy the delicate results."

Pam received her BFA and BEd in 1974. She set up a basement studio and taught pottery to school children and adults through the Halifax City school board until 1976, when we bought our building in Mahone Bay.

I started a pharmacy program in 1968 at Ohio Northern University, completing the first quarter of my third year before realizing I had to do something else. I already had enough hours to graduate with a liberal arts degree, so when I changed to the art department, I only had to take studio courses and hand in a portfolio at the end of term. Coming from a science background, I naively believed I would learn the rules to paint and draw. I was very curious to know why things were "good" and asked questions all the time.

I finally became really interested in pottery my last year in school but hadn't accumulated enough experience to start my own studio. The answer was to go back to school, hence my arrival at the Nova Scotia College of Art and Design. My instructor in Ohio had gone to graduate school with Walter Ostrom and suggested I study with him as a special student, a designation that allowed me to just work in the studio all the time. This is where I gained the basic skills and confidence I used during the next 25 years. The most valuable thing I received from Walter was a critical eye in looking at my own work, as well as an appreciation for cultural influences on historical ceramics. From Homer Lord, I learned how to see the potential in seemingly unrelated items (clock springs make great trimming tools).

Graduate school was difficult for me because I was trying to find my own direction and teach at the same time. I tried many different avenues before discovering the fascination with making slip-decorated earthenware pottery. The earthenware clay came from a local brick factory, the definition of plastic clay, perfect for the wheel and a joy to work with.

After having met in the studio, Pam and I fell in love with each other and each other's pots, and decided to marry and set up a studio together. In 1976 we were

Birth Plates. Feathered and trailed colored slips on a white slipped earthenware clay. Transparent glaze fired to cone 03. Pam Birdsall.

both teaching and dreaming about our own studio. After looking at several properties "out in the country," we stumbled on the building we still occupy today. We really hadn't intended being in a town, but as soon as we saw the property, we instantly saw the potential.

We were able to arrange the financing to buy the building and we had already accumulated all of the necessary equipment but had no money left over for renovation. The building had been abandoned and needed a fair amount of immediate repair to make it habitable both as a studio and residence. We had to fix up a working studio, a showroom, and a place to live. The building needed wiring, plumbing, and insulation throughout. We were reluctant to get into more debt than we already had with a mortgage. It seemed most government programs were focused on providing large amounts of money to people who were creating large numbers of jobs. That definitely was not our intent, so we had to look elsewhere. Pam's father came to our rescue. We became a limited company and he sold redeemable shares of stock to a number of businessmen and friends. These people were very supportive and sympathetic to a young business trying to get started. This turned out to be just enough money, along with our own labor, to get the studio up and running. In five years we bought back all the shares.

Funding turned out to be the easiest problem to solve. We had all the equipment we needed and enough technical skill to begin developing our unique style. Learning about the difficulties of applying slip decora-

tion to unfired wet pots and the relationship humidity plays, had a long learning curve. This particular process doesn't tolerate mistakes and didn't give us any breaks. Then there were the challenges of creating a coherent body of work in the showroom. There were compromises between making the pots we wanted to make and the time it would take to decorate them. Thrown into the mix was the business end of pottery. Neither of us had any business training and knew nothing about bookkeeping, bill paying, invoicing, packing, or advertising. We had jumped in at the deep end, leaving our teaching jobs behind, and had to swim for it. Even faced with all these difficulties, there was never any doubt in our minds that we could do it. We had a confidence in our work and our ability to overcome any problem that arose. As storybook as it sounds, this perspective has served us well over the years.

We initially sold our pots from our own shop as well as wholesaling around the Maritime provinces and across Canada. We went to provincial trade shows in Halifax, allowing us to make the necessary contacts with various shop owners. Even though we only received half the retail price, it was money we could count on and would give us a wide exposure until people knew we were located in Mahone Bay. We were unwavering in our desire to make slip-decorated earthenware, and after three years of wholesaling, we realized several things. Initially, we had no idea what a great location Mahone Bay was and how many people came

Photo by Mary Dixon.

Flower Plate. Sgraffito and colored transparent glazes over a white slipped earthenware plate. Fired to cone 03. 30 cm diameter. Tim Worthington.

Photo by Mary Dixon.

Leaf Plate. Sgraffito, colored slips, and colored transparent glazes over white slipped earthenware plate. Fired to cone 03. 30.5 cm diameter. Tim Worthington.

Wisteria Jardiniére. Sponged blue slip, sgraffito, and colored transparent glazes over white slipped earthenware clay. Fired to cone 03. 16.5 cm high. Tim Worthington.

through the town during the summer. We also realized that slip decorating was not the best technique for wholesaling. The process was much too labor intensive and unforgiving, being totally affected by humidity, which changes frequently along the coast.

At this same time, blending with Pam's love of fashion, she developed a line of clay earrings that could be cast in a white clay and glazed with colored transparent glazes. This was a much better item for wholesaling. They were essentially unaffected by humidity and were so easy to pack compared to pottery. We could fill our orders in days instead of weeks and could teach our shopkeeper to make them, making her time much more productive.

Over the years we had three agents in Canada and also ventured into the export market in the U.S. with agents selling along the New England coast. Initially, this worked out well, but although the earrings were unique and visually appealing, the agents needed more diversity as well as higher priced items so that their time would be rewarded with higher commissions. We then made a conscious choice to concentrate more on our retail location rather than creating more things for wholesale. We were in a prime tourist area and found that we could sell all the pottery we could make. People liked the "different look" the slipware had and, more importantly, liked the changes in our work as we developed new ideas—our voice.

The summer was very busy, but the rest of the time (other than at Christmas) was pretty slow. We needed something to carry us on either side of the summer traffic. We had always loved the 17th century slip-trailed plates by the English Toft family, so commemorative plates for births, weddings, and anniversaries became our focus. This was such a nice connection with ceramic tradition as well as becoming a part of people's lives. Pam developed a slip-decorated design of a duck family for the center of the plates. The first child's plate would have three ducks—mother, father, and baby—with the baby's name and birth date on the rim. When the second baby was born, a plate with four ducks representing the mother, father, first baby, and the new baby would be made. We now have those children ordering plates for their own children! Many families have given the plates to all of their children and grandchildren, documenting their births in one of the oldest and most permanent of materials. In a time of mass production, computer designing, and instant results, people really appreciate an item that has taken time and skill to produce. And to receive something that has been custom-made for them is becoming increasingly unique.

However, we also recognize and employ some of these amazing "new" tools, using both computers and digital cameras. The computer has been a fast way to do various layouts for printed materials, brochures, signs, product cards, and advertising. The most recent tools

Commemorative Plate. Plate thrown with a local brown earthenware clay. Feathered color slips on a white slip. Carved letters and transparent colored glaze. Fired to cone 03. 40 cm diameter. Pam Birdsall and Tim Worthington.

we use are e-mails and the Internet. Our Web site is used as a catalog for our commemorative plates and e-mail is perfect for clarification of orders. The digital camera can take an image that can then be posted on the Web page within hours. I find it somewhat ironic that we are using this instant communication to obtain information to produce something that has been made in virtually the same way for thousands of years.

We both truly believe that after 25 years the process of making pottery can be used as a metaphor for life. We have come to understand that change is constantly presented for you to make choices and act upon. If the pot collapses, is dropped, knocked over, glaze runs, kiln overfires, pot cracks, kiln wash falls in the middle of a plate, you simply make another one. You focus on what worked and what didn't work in the piece and take it to the next step.

We waited six years to get the pottery established before having our two children. Sam and Claire brought time and its organization into a totally new light. The act of making pottery taught our children that a new idea can formulate in the imagination, be discussed, drawn out, prototypes made and revised, and then finally realized as a physical object in the shop. They also understand that this magic transformation, the realization of a thought form, *can* happen and takes both time and effort, a very empowering

concept for a young person. Having them grow up with both of us in the studio all the time has made Sam and Claire aware of the constant changes pottery goes through and those parallels with life. They have seen the opportunity those changes have presented for making positive choices.

We recognized the changes in our relationship over time and realized we worked better as creative partners than as husband and wife. We still remain the best of friends, business partners, each other's best critic, and loving parents to our children.

Our advice to people starting out is to have the confidence and believe in your own talent and vision. Things will not happen overnight. Be patient and accumulate the necessary experience. Develop your business skills, prepare a plan, and remember that the plan requires you to do the work. Computer skills can be a real time saver and time is, after all, your most important commodity. It determines to a great extent what kind of work you will ultimately make. Remember to laugh and see the bigger picture. You can't be prepared for everything that will come your way, so your ability to deal with change in a positive, constructive way is essential to the survival of the creative artist.

Birdsall-Worthington Pottery Ltd., PO Box 367, Mahone Bay, Nova Scotia, Canada B0J 2E0, e-mail: bwpot@bwr.eastlink.ca., Web site: www.pottery.ns.ca.

Sponged Bowl. Feathered and sponged colored slips on a white slipped earthenware clay. Transparent glazes fired to cone 03. 28 cm diameter. Pam Birdsall.

Covered Bowl. Brushed colored slips on a white slipped earthenware clay. Transparent glaze, fired to cone 03. 15 cm high. Pam Birdsall and Tim Worthington.

Blue Rimmed Plate. Feathered colored slips on a white slipped earthenware clay. Transparent blue and clear glaze. Fired to cone 03. 34 cm diameter. Pam Birdsall.

Chapter 6

Financial Considerations

by Sharon Williams, Accountant

When operating a business, you have an obligation to keep an accurate set of books, whether you do them yourself or hire someone to do them for you. A set of books keeps track of your money, both income and outgo. When starting out in a new business, finances can be very tight, so you may want to start your own set of books. If you have a computer, you can purchase one of many choices of computer business or simple accountancy programs to assist you, or you can purchase a journal, ledger, or accounting book, and record your expenses in columns. How many categories you have to report controls how many columns you will need in your book when you purchase it. A 12-column ledger is fairly standard for most small businesses. You should have a column for income and taxes (if applicable) and then the different types of expenses, depending on your particular media of work. For example: Materials purchased to make your artwork, Advertising and Promotions, Accounting and Bookkeeping, Automobile Expenses, Bank Charges and Interest, Insurance, Office Supplies, Rent, Repairs and Maintenance, Telephone, Travel, Utilities, and Wages. These are just a few examples of what type of headings you may have.

If you would like more detailed information, break it down further. A word of caution: Don't let your bookkeeping fall behind, because the bigger the pile becomes the more likely it is that you are not going to process it. Keep all receipts, large and small, and put a little note on them if they are not self-explanatory. This helps greatly if you are ever audited. File in months so if you ever need to retrieve the invoice or receipt you don't have to go through the whole pile. At the end of a year you must take an inventory of your products for sale, your work in progress, and your raw materials. They are calculated at what it would cost to replace them. This information can then be summarized and reported. You will need to report your information to the authorities once a year in the form of a Balance Sheet and an Income Statement. Your Balance Sheet will cover assets such as your cash in the bank, amounts owed to you, and equipment you have. It also covers your Liabilities such as what you may owe for supplies, taxes, and bank loans. The next section of

your Balance Sheets depends on whether you are a proprietor or an incorporated company. If you are self-employed, the next section is Owner's Equity, which covers how much money you have put into the business and how much you have taken out, and what has been left from previous years. This calculates your owner's equity. If you are an incorporated company, it would also cover how many shares and what kind of shares, common, preferred, voting, and nonvoting. It also covers, if stocks and bonds, what types and how many are actually issued. This section is called Shareholders Equity.

The next document is your Income Statement, which covers the income and expenses your business has had over the past year. When recording your transactions always put income with income and expense with expense. Auditors like to see debits with debits (expenses) and credits with credits (income).

As your business grows you may have to pass tasks to other staff, which may include financial responsibilities. This makes it necessary to control theft, fraud, and errors made by people within the company. There are a number of established accounting principles that have been designed to provide internal controls over cash. You should deposit all your cash and checks, then pay by your company check. This helps in calculating your income and expenses properly. If you sometimes need small amounts of cash, set up a petty cash system with $25. If you are replacing money often, increase the amount. To replace your funds in petty cash, add up all the receipts and write the check for that amount. The check and remaining cash should add up to your original amount. Have all your invoices prenumbered to make it easier for you to show that all your income is accounted for (your tax auditor will like to see that you are not putting money in your own pocket). And, finally, reconcile your bank account. Should you have any errors they need to be corrected within a certain time frame (usually 30 days). It is most important to keep your tax filings up-to-date and put money aside to cover these expenses. The top reason for people going bankrupt is falling behind in taxes.

Whether you are a proprietor, partnership, or incorporated company, you must have a set of books.

For tax reasons they are treated differently, but not in recording the actual expenses.

You are a proprietorship or self-employed person when you work under your own name or a registered name and all your income is taxed under your name. This can sometimes put you in a higher tax bracket than you desire. If this is the case, you may want to incorporate your business and pay yourself a wage, and let the company pay the taxes on your behalf. This will put you and your company in a lower tax bracket. The other benefit to having a company is the legal liability. The corporation is separate from its owners. It has the right to sue and can be sued by others. In a partnership or proprietorship, the owners are not separate from the business.

There are two types of business corporations, private and public. A private business corporation is limited in the number of shareholders it can have and in the way it raises capital. It cannot have more than 50 shareholders and it must obtain its funds privately. It cannot sell shares or bonds to the public. Many small proprietorships and partnerships change their form of ownership to a private corporation in order to take advantage of the limited liability feature of the corporation. The owners still control and own the business, yet have protection for their personal assets. A public corporation is a business corporation that can have any number of shareholders. It can sell shares and bonds to the public. When dealing with the legal matters of your business you would be wise to have a lawyer to help in making your decisions.

Which brings me to contracts (see also Chapter 5: Legal Considerations). You would be wise to get a contract when consigning your work at other locations. This will outline what is expected from you and what is expected from them. Does it include advertising or is this your expense? What about the tax obligations and does your commission include taxes? I would not hesitate to hire a lawyer to do a quick perusal of any contract before you sign it. I have learned that this is money well spent.

Another topic to be considered is insurance. If you have a shop on your premises, liability insurance is a must in case of an accident on your property. You wouldn't want to go to a lot of work just to have one accident take it all away from you. Another is personal disability insurance. The cost of such insurance depends on the length of time before you can start claiming. For example, you may want your insurance to kick in 30 days after you can no longer work due to illness or injury. Or you may have three months of savings to cover the monthly bills and can wait a while before your insurance starts covering you. If you can wait the three months, your insurance premiums will be greatly reduced. Another aspect would be how long the insurance will pay out. I always ask clients how much time is left before their mortgage is paid out and how long it would it take to retrain them for a different career. These are all factors in considering how long you would need your insurance to pay out.

The task of setting up a new business can seem daunting and overwhelming. You can choose to do it all yourself or find a good support group of professionals to help you along your way. Thoughtful and careful planning can mean the difference between making a successful living from your art and surviving the ever-changing world around you. Businesses that are disorganized are more likely to do the opposite and often fail.

Good luck in all your endeavors.

Sharon Williams, Accountant, 2921 Dickerson Place, Victoria, B.C., Canada V9B 2G8, e-mail: s.w.accounting@shaw.ca.

Chapter 7

Achieving Visibility in the Art World

by Polly Beach, Editor/Publisher, Clay Times *magazine*

On the path to success as a visual artist, the road to widespread recognition is often the least traveled. This is not necessarily because visibility is a difficult thing to achieve. Rather, many artists are just too shy to promote themselves, or they are simply unaware of the many valuable ways to utilize print, radio, and television media for gaining recognition of their work and its association with their name.

Free Publicity

In most cases, exposure of one's artistic accomplishments via the media costs little if anything at all. Many different avenues for this type of exposure exist, including the press release, listings in special events columns, critics' reviews in the art section of newspapers, journals, or magazines, artist interviews, and feature stories.

PRESS RELEASE

Baltimore Clayworks
5707 Smith Avenue
Baltimore, MD 21209
Phone (410) 578-1919
Fax (410) 578-0058
www.baltimoreclayworks.org

Media Contact: Leigh Taylor Mickelson
Program Director
(410) 578-1919 ext 18
Date: May 30, 2002
Email: leigh.mickelson@baltimoreclayworks.org
FOR IMMEDIATE RELEASE through 8/31/02

Baltimore Clayworks presents

Silos, Stables and Dining-room Tables
A Solo Exhibition featuring the work of
Bernadette Curran
Lormina Salter Fellowship Recipient, 2001-02

Baltimore Clayworks is proud to present *Silos, Stables and Dining-room Tables*; showcasing the whimsical functional ceramic works of Bernadette Curran, our 2001-02 Lormina Salter Fellowship Recipient. The exhibition will feature a culmination of work from her year-long residency in the Clayworks studio community. Visitors will be treated to a menagerie of barnyard livestock; chickens, horses, cows and more promenading as salt and pepper sets, sugar and creamers and covered dishes. The show runs August 3rd to 31st, with an opening reception on Saturday, August 3rd from 6 – 8pm (admission is free).

Ms. Curran was raised in the heart of Pennsylvania Dutch Country where she developed an appreciation for the inherent beauty and craftsmanship in a hand-made object. She is especially inspired by the region's Folk Art which "quietly teaches the virtue of patience and application; made of honest materials, they are sturdy hand-made objects of years long past." When creating her wheel-thrown and altered pots she is intrigued by the "thrill of altering a pot out of the round [which] creates a playful environment for the barn structures, farm animals and the services they prompt at the dining room table. The carved and drawn surfaces function decoratively, but suggest elements of narrative and traces of moments remembered."

Baltimore Clayworks is a not-for-profit ceramic art center located in the Mt. Washington neighborhood in northwest Baltimore. Founded in 1980, Clayworks is housed in two renovated buildings across the street from each other, and offers classes, artists' spaces, exhibitions and programs in the community. **Hours are 10AM - 5 PM, Monday through Saturday. For more information call Baltimore Clayworks at 410-578-1919.**

The Press Release

The press release is usually a one or two page news announcement that is faxed, e-mailed, or mailed to several media organizations at the same time. Topics worthy of an artist's press release could be:

- advance word of a new studio opening or an upcoming gallery exhibition;
- follow-up summary of a fundraiser or special art sale;
- announcement of new awards, honors, or special achievements of the artist (i.e., art works just purchased for the White House collection).

The press release should be written in the third person narrative with the most important information at the beginning and less important details at the end. The writer should keep the audience in mind and tailor the announcement to answer their questions: Who? What? Where? When? Why? How?

The top of the press release should include a release date (preferred date of publication) and contact information (name of the person to contact and their telephone number and e-mail address). Below, the headline should be centered in bold face type or all upper case letters. The first paragraph should open with the location of the news in capital letters (i.e., "WASHING-TON, D.C. — The Smithsonian has announced the procurement of a new collection of ancient artifacts", etc.). At the very end of the announcement, the notation ### or -30- (standard newsroom lingo for "the end") should appear to indicate that the information is complete. It's a good idea to double space the entire document to enhance readability and allow the editor to jot notes between lines.

Special Events Listings

Most local newspapers feature free listings to which readers can turn for details on upcoming events. Advance deadlines for such listings can vary from a few days for a daily or weekly newspaper to many months for a monthly or bimonthly magazine. The artist should research the publications in his or her area and note their event listing deadlines, then provide timely information on any of the following scenarios:

• advance word of the artist's open house or seasonal sale to be held individually or with a group of fellow artists;
• announcement of an upcoming art/craft fair, including names of participants, type of goods to be sold, planned entertainment, and other information designed to draw the public (include time, date, location, and admission fees, if any);
• advance word of a gallery opening or exhibit.

It's good to submit copies of the event press release to different members of the same media organization: i.e., the news director, the events editor, editor of the arts pages, etc. This way, if one editor has no room to place it, one of the others might. Better yet, all of them could feasibly publish details of the press release in different sections of their publication at different times, offering much greater publicity. If the artist has access to a computer with a database program, a file containing the names, addresses, submission deadlines, and other relevant contact information on media representatives can be created for use whenever necessary.

Critics' Reviews

There's usually an art critic on staff at every major metropolitan newspaper, and most art journals, magazines, etc. When holding a gallery or museum exhibit, it's advisable for the artist to send out as many invitations to the opening as possible to art critics, curators, gallery owners, and other important members of the arts community, as well as to fellow artists.

If invitations are personalized with a handwritten note and signature (i.e., "Hope to see you there—Robin"), recipients feel special and are more likely to

attend. Hopefully, the art critic will be so impressed by the show that he or she will give it a great write-up. (Even if the write-up isn't favorable, publicity of the show will make the name of the artist and the works much more recognizable, and the constructive criticism could help further the artist's creative advancement.)

Artist Interviews

Whenever a special event is coming up, the artist may further promote his or her work by arranging one-on-one interviews with local radio stations, cable television companies, and in the case of high-profile events, the national media. Radio and television companies love to pepper the day's disturbing news with good news, and anything having to do with art is almost always good news.

This is a scenario where an artist who is active in local art organizations (i.e., craft guilds, museum committees, etc.) can serve as spokesperson for the overall event and earn a few free minutes of air time by granting an interview for a news clip. Invariably, in identifying the artist to the general public, the interviewer will offer general information about the artist and his or her work, again adding to name recognition and familiarity with the body of art being produced.

Feature Stories

Perhaps the best free publicity the artist can hope for is a full-length feature story on his or her work, especially if it involves a cover photo in a popular publication. To be considered for such an honor, the artist should maintain a portfolio of high-quality images of his or her work, studio, exhibitions, creative processes, and any other visuals that might be of interest to potential readers. If the portfolio is updated twice yearly, it will remain current and available for the artist to distribute on short notice.

It's important for the artist to determine what makes his or her work or creative process unique and different from what others are doing, and how readers could benefit from learning his/her story. This unique quality can then be transformed into a "slant," or special topic designed to be appealing because of its uniqueness. Once the artist has a "slant" in mind for his/her proposed feature story, it's time to create an outline to be submitted with a query letter to the editor of the publication in which the artist hopes to be profiled.

The Query Letter

This is a brief, one-page letter on letterhead. It introduces the artist and his/her work, and describes what makes them unique and of potential interest to readers. Details include:

- brief background information on the artist, including relevant education and work experience;
- listings of special achievements/honors and organizational affiliations that lend greater credibility to the artist and his/her work;
- a summary of the proposed article and why it would be of interest to publication readers;
- writer contact information (name, address, work and home telephone, e-mail, and Web site address for supplementary information, if applicable).

It's important that the writer of the article is skilled and experienced. If the artist does not have strong writing abilities, it's advisable to seek out a professional writer to do the story (as well as to write the query letter and story outline). While a professional writer can respectably praise the artist within the story, the artist who writes their own story could be considered self-aggrandizing if they praise themselves in writing. As a rule, if the artist can write well, he or she should stick to how-to articles or commentaries; oth-

erwise, it's usually better for a professional writer to do the story.

The Proposal Outline

Most periodicals maintain a list of writer's guidelines that describe specific requirements for editorial and photographic submissions. These can be requested by mail or e-mail, or found on the publication's Web site. After review of these guidelines, the writer should draft the proposal outline to provide specific information on the story topic, tailored to the needs of the publication. The proposal outline should include an introduction and conclusion, with relative information broken into segments in between.

Feature Submission Requirements

Along with the query letter and the proposed story outline, it's a good idea for the artist to submit:

- sample images related to the story (12 to 24 previously unpublished images. *Never* submit the same images to more than one publication);
- copies of published articles about the artist;
- the artist's biography;
  - an artist's statement (brief description of his/her work and feelings about the work) and listings of where finished works may be viewed and purchased;
  - self-addressed, stamped envelope (SASE) for return of materials.

Once the story has been accepted by the editor, the writer should complete the article within the agreed-upon time frame. Before submitting the story to the editor, it should be spell-checked and corrected. It's also a good idea to ask a few others to read the story for clarity, and make any necessary advance corrections.

The final story should then be submitted with:

- a computer disk with the story saved as a text only, RTF (rich text format), or ASCII Delimited Text file (these file formats are readable by almost any computer);
- a printout of the story and photo captions;
- any additional photos, etc. obtained since the proposal outline was submitted.

The Importance of Photographic Images

Submission of high-quality photographic images is a must for getting pub-

---

Making a Coiled Clay Pot

I. Introduction

    A. The history of handbuilt clay pots

    B. How coil pots can be used in today's household

II. How-to process

    A. Forming the base (illustrate with Fig. 1)

    B. Rolling the coils (illustrate with Fig. 2)

    C. Attaching the coils (illustrate with Fig. 3)

    D. Drying (illustrate with Fig. 4)

    E. Decorating (illustrate with Fig. 5)

    F. Firing (illustrate with Fig. 6)

III. Conclusion

    A. Alternative materials for forming and decorating

    B. References (books, magazines, Web sites) for
    more information on making coil pots

A sample outline for a how-to article on making a coiled clay pot.

lished. No matter how talented the artist, their work will most likely be rejected if it is depicted in a poor-quality slide, print, or digital image.

Following are some of the most important qualities editors seek out when selecting images for publication:

- Sharp focus and good depth of field. The quality of any professional publication depends heavily on the quality of the photographs; therefore, editors want to publish only those images that are crisp, clear, and well-composed. For three-dimensional artwork, the photographer should focus on the front of the subject and adjust aperture/shutter speed to obtain the best depth of field possible. In the case of traditional photographs, it's advisable to use a slow-speed film (ASA/ISO 64 for slides; ASA/ISO 100 for prints) to prevent graininess. A tripod is recommended to allow for optimum depth of field.
- Neutral background. Professional product photographers know to select backdrop colors that don't interfere with the subject or complicate the photographic composition. Black, white, gray, and gradations of these tones (preferably provided by seamless photo paper backdrops) make the art stand out and offer the publication designer greater flexibility for page layouts with more than one photograph.
- High-quality resolution. Digital photos must be submitted at a high enough resolution (measured in dpi, dots per inch) so print quality is not jeopardized. At publication size (for example, 4" by 5") the minimum image resolution should be 300 dpi (that's twice the line screen normally used by professional color printers). In most cases, it's advisable to use the highest resolution available when shooting with a digital camera. Traditional photos should be scanned at a size of about 9" by 12" at 300 dpi to allow flexibility for use as a full-page photograph in a standard 8½" by 11" publication (slightly larger than print size to allow for paper trim around the edges). Digital images are most desirable when saved as TIFF format, although JPEG formats are also acceptable and can be converted by the publication art department. Black-and-white images should be saved as "grayscale"; color photographs should be saved as "CMYK" images.
- Accurate color rendition. Especially with digital photos, the artist needs to be certain that any image submitted for publication provides accurate color of the object depicted. Otherwise, the editor has no way of knowing if the color is correct. Ideally, before submission for publication, the artist will ask a local professional photographer/graphic designer to "color correct" the digital image on a calibrated (color-accu-

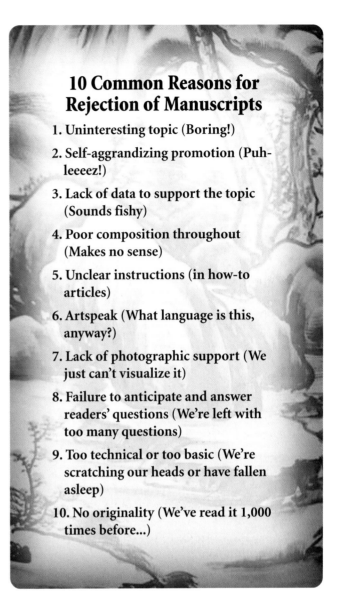

10 Common Reasons for Rejection of Manuscripts

1. Uninteresting topic (Boring!)
2. Self-aggrandizing promotion (Puh-leeeez!)
3. Lack of data to support the topic (Sounds fishy)
4. Poor composition throughout (Makes no sense)
5. Unclear instructions (in how-to articles)
6. Artspeak (What language is this, anyway?)
7. Lack of photographic support (We just can't visualize it)
8. Failure to anticipate and answer readers' questions (We're left with too many questions)
9. Too technical or too basic (We're scratching our heads or have fallen asleep)
10. No originality (We've read it 1,000 times before...)

rate) monitor, providing actual art works for comparison during that color correction process.

- Good exposure. Photos with an overall yellowish cast from incandescent lighting or a greenish cast from fluorescent lighting are not desirable for publication. These situations can be avoided with on-the-spot correction during the photo shoot by the use of special film and/or camera filters. Overexposed (too light) or underexposed (too dark) images can be avoided by "bracketing" when shooting: that is, shooting at the setting called for by the light meter as well as at two settings above and two settings below.
- Avoidance of "hot spots" and dark, sharp shadows. Ideally, art photos should show as much detail of the subject as possible. Harsh lighting that results in bright white reflections, or hot spots, yields distracting photos. Sharp, dark shadows can also block out details and detract from the image depicted. Ideally, the photographer will soften the lighting conditions with reflective devices when shooting so that both

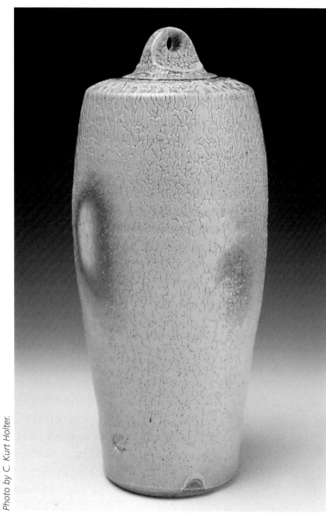

Photo by C. Kurt Holter.

Storage Jar by Bill van Gilder. 15" high x 6" wide. Gray stoneware wood-fired to cone 11. Lightly salt-glazed crackle slip with flashing.

reflections and shadows are muted. (Photographs taken outdoors on an overcast day can usually easily satisfy these requirements.)

- Good composition. Preferably, one artwork per photo should be depicted, unless the art itself is intended to be viewed as a series. There should be plenty of empty background space around all sides of the subject to give a "clean" look and allow more flexibility in layout. At the same time, however, it's important to fill most of the frame with the art subject, without making the frame look too cramped.

- Identification. Each image submitted should be identified with the name of the photographer (for a photo credit) along with the title of the work depicted (or "untitled," if there is none), name of the artist, dimensions of the work in inches or centimeters in international publications (height x width x depth), type of materials and processes used to create the work, and any other relevant information. Number the slide and use a separate reference sheet for captions, if necessary. The label should be placed on the front of the slide mount, with an arrow pointing upward to indicate where the top of the image is. Prints should be labeled on the back (refrain from writing directly on the photo). Digital images should be titled descriptively and referenced in a separate photo captions list. Ideally, each image will be provided with a full photo caption to identify special details of the work the reader might not otherwise guess from looking at the photo.

The photo at left offers an ideal example of the type of image coveted by publishers of fine art. It features crisp, clear focus and good depth of field, a neutral, uncluttered background with "breathing space" around the subject, softened shadows and softened highlights, and quality resolution and proper exposure.

- Good variety of images. For a feature story, it's best for the editor to have a wide selection from which to choose. One to two dozen images of the artist's best works relating to the theme of the article allow the editor and graphic designer more creative possibilities for presentation on the printed page. Images depicting the artist at work, the artist's studio, home, and/or teaching environment, the artist's work in progress, and the artist's finished works on display allow for an in-depth look into the creative process. If slides are submitted, they are best placed in plastic slide sheets that hold 20 images per page (again, these should be labeled or referenced with captions and relevant information discussed above). Color prints may be placed in envelopes and labeled with captions on the back.

Macintosh and PC computers are now equipped with CD-Rom drives and both platforms can read CDs, which can store multiple high-quality images.

If At First You Don't Succeed...

It may take several submissions of press releases, event announcements, gallery invitations, etc. before the artist begins to achieve visibility through the media. Yet every submission is an important contribution to the process of name recognition. Eventually, the accomplished artist who is persistent in promoting his or her work will attain the visibility he or she deserves. One must remember that persistence is the key.

Biographical Sketch
Kinichi Shigeno

Kinichi Shigeno.

It has been 30 years since I began working with clay, initially following the traditional way of becoming a potter in Japan. I graduated from high school in 1971 and entered a ceramic training institute in Seto, a pottery production center since the 9th century A.D. I majored in ceramic design and after graduating I tried to find a place to apprentice. I naively went to see Tokuro Kato, one of the most famous potters in Japan, and asked if he would take me on as an apprentice! I eventually got an apprenticeship with Masaru Kamei. His father was also a potter and he carried on the tradition normally expected in Japanese craft families. I spent the next seven years working for him, doing a variety of duties. In 1972, I was paid around $400 to $500 a month, probably more than most apprentices.

My experience as an apprentice differed greatly from what I learned in school. I learned a lot of theory about design, but I didn't have much experience using design theories with ceramics. During the day I spent my working time doing what Sensei asked me to do. This included hand building, using molds, glazing, firing, and wheelwork. The skills I learned through repetition enabled me to pursue my own projects. In Japan, competency in skills is paramount, creativity comes second. The thinking is that without the technical skills, creativity cannot be expressed. I think that in the western world, the creative process is emphasized more than the skills.

My experience was not in a large pottery factory but with a ceramic artist. What is unique about this sensei (teacher) and deshi (apprentice) relationship is the chance to see how one artist goes through the creative process, the preparation for exhibitions, how connections are made, both socially and creatively, and just

general ways on how to make a living. Being an apprentice was not all clay work. Sometimes I was the chauffeur, caddy, and babysitter. It was all in a day's work. More important to an apprentice was what was done at night, on their own time. This was where I developed and learned how to make my own pottery or style. Sometimes I felt that nothing would work out. However, my teacher encouraged me to enter various ceramic competitions, an important activity for an apprentice. Through these various juried exhibitions and competitions you start to establish yourself before you go out on your own. These shows are an important part of a potter's development and acceptance into the ceramic world, almost an indicator of whether you can strike out on your own and whether or not you show some kind of talent to be a ceramic artist. I was lucky enough to have my work accepted by the Asahi National Ceramic Competition and the Chuunichi International Ceramic Exhibition.

In 1980, after seven years as an apprentice, I decided to take the dramatic step to leave Seto and Japan. I applied to immigrate to Australia or Canada. Luckily the Canadian embassy connected me to an industrialist interested in establishing a pottery manufacturing plant in Vancouver. I moved to Kyushu, the southern island in Japan to prepare for this venture. For a year there I trained with another potter whose work was totally different from what I was used to doing. It was my first time working with porcelain and cobalt pigments.

A year later I was on a plane to Vancouver, full of optimism and excitement. As it turned out the project was not successful. When I left Japan I was given a one-way ticket and an immigrant visa. I decided to stay in

Vancouver and started to work for a local potter making earthy pottery, typical of the 1970s. The experience was valuable because I learned a lot about production pottery. However, I still knew nothing about how to sell my own work because the person I worked for had his own retail shop. At the same time, I built my own studio and continued to work on my own during the evenings. My new work was totally different, combining my cobalt design work and porcelain training in Kyushu with Canadian-type production work. I also began to use overglaze enamels.

I started selling my work at a craft co-op, gaining enough exposure that various retail shops began taking an interest. However, all of this did not translate into a full-time career at the start. It wasn't until 1987, almost four years later, that my work began to be noticed. I entered competitions and was part of many group exhibitions. One of the most important international competitions was the Faenza Ceramic Competition in Italy, regarded by many revered Japanese potters as the most important international ceramic competition to enter. I was beginning to build my professional resumé and credibility as an artist, a very important asset in being able to secure an exhibition in Tokyo at the renowned Takashima Department Store Gallery. Years later, I entered a competition to design place settings for the Lieutenant Governor's residence. To me this was more than a competition; it was a challenge to use design theory, production techniques, and creativity for an important project. It was also the first time I had ever attempted to make a place setting! Winning the competition and being in the exhibition gave me a lot of exposure and opportunities to sell and exhibit at various galleries. The various nominations for excellence in crafts that I received were in part due to this one competition. Many years later, the same place settings were used to host the Heads of State at the World Trade Summit in Vancouver.

My own studio has now been established for over 15 years. I try to balance what I consider production work with being an artist. Having a healthy production line gives me the financial stability to do exhibitions and to enter competitions. I find both aspects equally important. Being a ceramic artist is hard work. It is both physically and mentally challenging. If I were to give advice about becoming a potter, it would be to think beyond the production work. Even if one thinks that production work is boring, the creative challenge is always there.

Kinichi Shigeno, 9280 Chapman Crescent, Richmond, British Columbia, Canada V7E 1M5, e-mail: kshigeno@shaw.ca.

Photo by Kinichi Shigeno.

High-heeled Shoes. Porcelain. Casting and polychrome. 9½" x 12" x 4". 1994.

Teapot. Stoneware. Casting and polychrome. 16" x 16½" x 5½". 1997.

Bowl. Porcelain. Underglaze cobalt and polychrome. 18" x 8½". 2000.

Blue Bird Dinnerware. Thrown porcelain and oxide. Cups 4" and plates 11". 1991.

Biographical Sketch Robin Hopper and Judi Dyelle

Robin Hopper
and Judi Dyelle.

Photo by Morgan Saddington.

Robin Hopper

My personal journey to where I am today seems convoluted but started in South London, England. An early childhood, where German bombs of the Second World War left gaping wounds of blue clay from their destruction of people and property, also gave me my first love of clay as a material to play with. Residual memories of this material must have stayed with me when I became an art student in 1955, mainly doing drawing, painting, and printmaking. As a result of a summer job working in a pottery, where I wedged clay for eight hours a day, six days a week (chores that anyone in their right mind would probably have run away from!), I found that I was totally seduced by the cyclical nature of the medium, from malleable mud to hard-fired mug.

Before the development of acrylic paints, and physically nauseated by the smells of turpentine and oil paint in the painting studio, I changed direction to ceramics as my major in conjunction with theatre design and printmaking as my minors. After five years' study of art, I wanted to start my own studio. Before I had the cash necessary to buy property, I worked in theatre as an actor, stage manager, property maker, and set designer.

Having spent most of my late teenage summers hitchhiking in Continental Europe and being familiar with several languages, I also worked for seven summers as a travel guide taking tourists everywhere from Moscow to Madrid, Paris to Pisa, and from Stockholm to Seville. There are few places in Europe I haven't been. Being a travel guide gave me a good insight into people, tourism, cultural tourism, and business stemming from this source—valuable lessons for when I got my first studio going in a rural village, 60 miles west of London.

With the occasional help of winter work in theatre and summer work in tourism, my studio became firmly established in four years, and I was selling my work all over England quite quickly and becoming fairly successful. My approach to developing my business as an artist grew from observing both my parents' grocery business and the business of tourism. I have always maintained a mix of work from the production of functional ware for the masses to art works in clay for the aficionado.

After several successful years I felt the need for change, more space, and more challenge. With my young family I moved to Canada, initially to Toronto, where I had been offered a teaching job that I deemed necessary while organizing a studio in a new country. After five years of full-time teaching (with a second full-time job in my studio) the studio was able to fully support the family. Much as I love teaching, I quit, and relished the extra 30 hours per week I gained. From the way that my work and its marketing had developed since coming to my adopted country, I was convinced that being a full-time self-employed artist was not going to jeopardize my income and family security. It is now 30 plus years since I made that decision. After 10 years in Ontario, I couldn't tolerate the extremes of climate any more, so I looked toward the West Coast, found an old farm property just outside Victoria on Vancouver Island, rebuilt most of the house and the studio building, and started off in business once again.

After six years here, my first wife and I parted ways, and I was later joined by my second wife, Judi Dyelle. The business became a corporation titled 'Chosin Pottery Inc., a shortened version of the name Metchosin, the community that we are part of.

Since I have talked about my various approaches to

business throughout this book, and Judi manages the business side of our operation, it seems more logical for her to tell her story, both before and after we became partners.

Judi Dyelle

I never started out to be a potter, although I guess I should have paid attention to the old photograph of myself at age eight, sitting proudly in front of a board full of clay ashtrays I had just made. I had planned to be a physical education teacher, but as the fates would have it, I am not. After many moves around the country, I graduated from high school in 1962 and went to the Ontario College of Art in Toronto, for five years. I had thought that I should study drawing and painting, but I had an option in ceramics and the old love of the material flooded back. I transferred to the material arts department with my major in ceramics and a minor in metal work.

During my time in art school I realized that I would not be able to make a living as a potter right away, so I decided that I would teach. I enjoyed teaching, as I had done it from the age of 16 with children at summer camps. In my last year of school, it became evident that I needed to know more if I was to be a good teacher and I applied for a Canada Council Grant to study in Japan with Tatsuzo Shimaoka. I was fortunate to receive the grant and left for Japan the fall after my graduation (1967). I stayed in Japan for a year and a half. This was probably the most rewarding and memorable experience I have ever had. It had a major impact on my approach and understanding of ceramics. It certainly impacted on my methods of teaching. In Kyoto I was introduced to porcelain and fell in love with it immediately.

I returned to Toronto and started to substitute teach at a high school for the arts. I didn't have any money for a studio or equipment so I used the facilities at the school. I had also just become a mother so there wasn't very much extra time to be a potter too. After a year in the city, I moved to one of the western suburbs of Toronto and applied for and received a Local Initiatives Project Grant. This grant allowed me to purchase my first wheel, but still no studio. Two years later, with another child, we moved to Vancouver and a year and a half later I was in Montreal.

I started teaching at Montreal's Visual Arts Centre and later became the resident potter and head of the ceramic department. This was a great opportunity as it provided me with a much needed studio facility, a great place to sell my work, and allowed me to bring in a wide variety of ceramic artists to do workshops for my students and keep me abreast of what was going on in the ceramic field. The position allowed me to set my own timetable, which was very important now that I was a single parent. Slowly I began to establish my own home studio.

One of the artists invited to do a workshop for my students was Robin Hopper. I had met Robin earlier in Toronto, so when he came to Montreal we renewed our friendship, which over time eventually developed into a partnership and then marriage.

In 1981 I decided it was time to quit teaching and really try and make a go of it as a full-time potter. Well, life doesn't always go as planned and it was at this point that Robin decided to move to Montreal to be with me. The winter was too much for Robin and he decided that we should move back to Vancouver Island to take over his old studio. So with a leap of faith, I sold my house, packed a U-Haul truck, and we drove across the country to start a new adventure.

There were major adjustments upon arrival. I needed to make a new clay body, as the one I had used in Montreal was not available in the west. I had to learn to share my space with a very messy other half. This would be the first time that I would be responsible for selling my work from my own showroom. Thank heaven I had a father who was in retail all his life. By osmosis, I had picked up many valuable tips on marketing and promotion. It became evident from the beginning that I would be in charge of the business. Having a shop and trying to make pots is not the easiest situation and I found that the interruptions were getting to be too much. We were lucky that a fellow potter from Montreal, Arlene Yarnell, had moved to the area a year earlier and I approached her to see if she would like to work for us. She was delighted to come. We got a Manpower Grant to train her to throw some of the smaller production items, make clay and glazes, and take care of the shop. She has been with us now for 13 years and I don't know what we would do without her.

To stimulate the public into buying art pottery and make them aware that we were open for business, we started two special events, our annual sale the last weekend in November and "Fired Up—Contemporary Works in Clay" on the last weekend in May, an event with 14 of British Columbia's best-known potters. Both of these have been going strong for 18 years now and are much anticipated.

As the business grew, we realized we needed a better space to display the more artistic pieces. We decided that a real gallery should be added to the showroom. It has a total of 1,000 square feet of display where we sell upwards of 95% of our work direct retail. It is surrounded by a spectacular two-and-a-half-acre, award-winning garden of Robin's design. Beneath the gallery is my studio. Peace at last! We also found that we needed another employee, part-time. Shana Watson has been a great help with Robin's glaze research, testing thousands of glazes for his other books. She is also "Queen of the Koi," making large tiles in the shape and colors of Japanese carp for garden use.

We are fortunate that we live in an area that is home to numerous artists in all media. Since we live in a rural area, this has helped to interest more people to come and explore the different studios. Robin and I have both felt that it is important to develop a place that is a "destination" to attract people to visit. We want to give a total experience and share the very special environment we call home.

'Chosin Pottery Inc., 4283 Metchosin Rd., Victoria, British Columbia, Canada V9C 3Z4, phone (250) 474-2676, e-mail: chosin@chosinpottery.ca, Web site: www.chosinpottery.ca.

Photo by Janet Dwyer.

Large Plate - Dark Garden Series. Cone 10 reduction fired porcelain. Multiple glaze application with brushwork and trailed glazes. Robin Hopper.

"Kamloops Series" Boat. Wheel thrown and altered porcelain, high fired reduction to cone 9. Judi Dyelle.

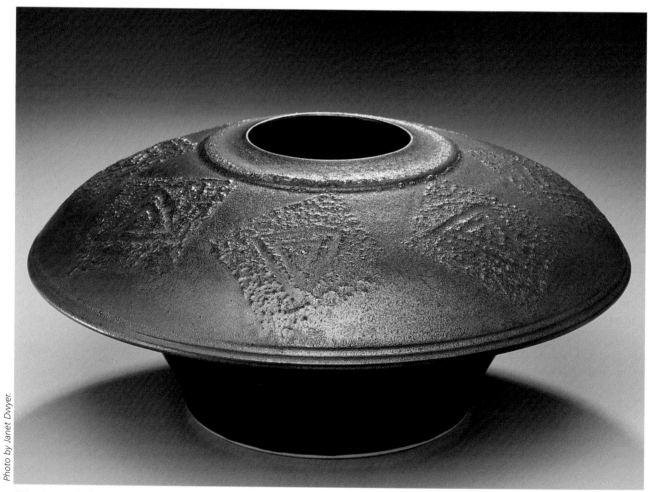

"Kamloops Series" Paracas Vase. Wheel thrown and assembled porcelain, high fired reduction to cone 9. Judi Dyelle.

Basket Form - Clematis Series. Porcelain, cone 10 reduction. Multiple glaze application plus brushwork. Robin Hopper.

Photo by Janet Dwyer.

Vase. Porcelain with trailed slip and turquoise glaze over. Cone 8 oxidation fired. Robin Hopper.

Lidded Jar. Cone 10 reduction fired porcelain. Dry-matt shino glaze and brushwork in iron oxide. Robin Hopper.

Photo by Janet Dwyer.

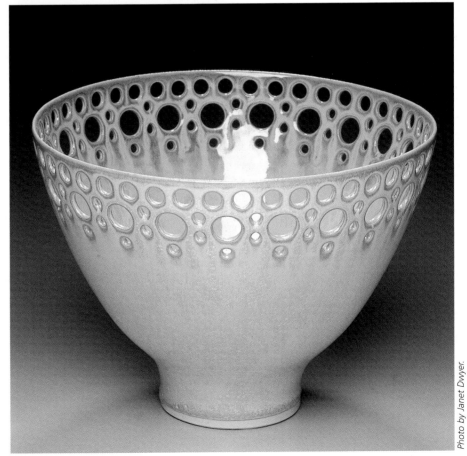

"Crystal Pink Series" Pierced Bowl. Wheel thrown porcelain, high fired reduction to cone 10. Judi Dyelle.

Photo by Janet Dwyer.

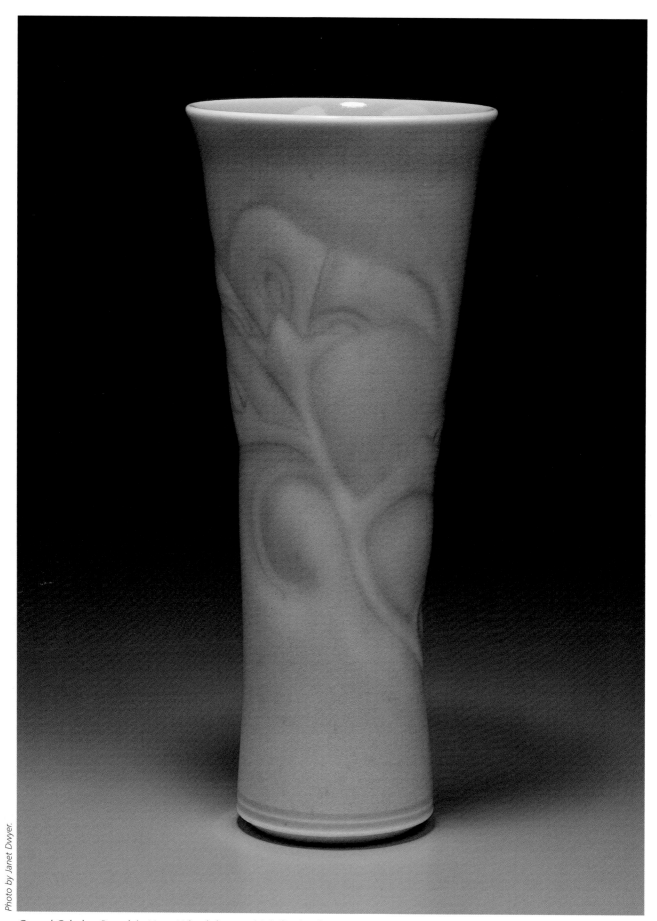

Carved Celadon Porcelain Vase. Wheel thrown, high fired reduction to cone 10. Judi Dyelle.

Chapter 8

Photographing Works of Art

By Janet Dwyer, fine art product photographer

While a photographic record of your artwork is desirable to chart personal growth, it soon becomes a requirement for self-promotion. High-quality shots are essential for gallery or juried show acceptance, brochures, publications, and Internet use. The question then becomes whether to do your own photography or to hire a professional.

Although photographer's rates vary considerably and may seem expensive, remember that hiring a professional can justify itself very quickly, leading to increased positive exposure and direct sales. Consider that gallery curators, show jurors, and potential buyers will judge your work by what they see in a photograph; doors can close if they don't like the view!

Working With a Professional Photographer

If you decide to hire a professional photographer, look for someone who specializes in shooting art or is a competent product photographer; ask other artists, galleries, or the local museum who they use. View the photographer's portfolio, especially their work in your medium.

Discuss final costs, negative ownership, copyright, and other issues upfront. Before work begins, have all these issues detailed in a document signed by both you and the photographer. Shooting several pieces in one session can reduce costs (some photographers specify a minimum number).

For economy, get all of your needs covered initial-

Illustrating perspective and viewpoint. The photo on the left was taken with a 55 mm lens from a slightly higher angle than the one on the right, which was shot with a 105 mm lens from farther away. The left photo shows more depth. Objects will appear compressed as the subject-to-camera distance increases and the camera viewpoint will emphasize certain forms more than others. Ceramic teapot set by Diane Burt.

ly (extra slide copies, digital format or larger prints). If the end use of the photographs will be limited edition prints, giclee, posters, or high-quality reproductions, have the photographer shoot large format transparency film (4" by 5") for sharper, less grainy reproduction.

Doing Your Own Photography

If you decide to do your own photography, consider the best use of your time, your budget, and ask yourself these questions.

Is your artwork easy or difficult to shoot? Flat, nonglossy art is easier than most media. Jewelry and glasswork are often the most challenging. Highly textured or larger scale adds to the difficulty.

Do you have reliable equipment and clean space? The basic requirement is a 35 mm manual camera with interchangeable lenses in the 35 to 105 mm focal range. If you need to purchase equipment and decide to buy used instead of new, purchase good quality equipment (Pentax Spotmatic or K series, Nikon FM/FE2) from a reputable dealer, both for the warranty and operating advice. If your artwork is small scale, look for a 100 mm macro lens, which allows greater subject-to-camera distance than a 50mm, allowing easier access for positioning of art.

The subject-to-camera distance, determined by your choice of lens, will also influence perspective, which is especially noticeable in groupings of items.

A wide angle lens (24 or 28 mm) may be needed if you are shooting large art or working in tighter spaces. The downside is that many wide angle lenses introduce unwanted distortion of perspective. Various other accessories are useful, making the process easier and the results more professional looking.

Should you use a digital camera or film? If you are shooting for Web site use only, consider using a digital camera. Check out www.dpreview.com or search "digital cameras" for recent reviews of current models in the two MP range and better. If you are not very computer literate, expect a steep learning curve and a major time commitment. If you have a scanner, you can scan existing slides or prints to the digital format but the reverse process, converting a digital file to a slide, will result in some loss of quality. The advantage of digital images is that they can be altered, retouched, and color balanced with a basic editing program like Photoshop Elements or Photoshop LE, then directly on the Web, e-mailed, or burned to a CD.

Digital imaging has definite requirements for decent quality. Resolution, measured in ppi (pixels per inch) or dpi (dots per inch), and the final size (the width and height of the image) are the factors to consider. If the image will be printed at a photo lab or used

Accessories include silver foil tape for masking slides, slides with computer printed labels, black presentation matt for slides, Kodak Color Control Patches and Gray Scale, Gray Card for metering, notebook, cable release, Formica and seamless paper background samples, tiles, black velvet, white gloves, brush, ear syringe blower, scissors, archival tape, foam core, foil boards, white boards, filters, level, jewelers cloth, lens cleaning cloth, clamps, picture hangers, felt pads, Hold It and beeswax for propping small objects.

for publication, at least 300dpi at the final size is required. However, it is best to check with your printer because resolution and file size are dependent on their output device. Image editing programs allow resizing or resampling of a file by interpolating the existing data. When enlarged or resampled up, pixels are randomly added and at a certain point the digital image will appear pixilated (you will start to notice individual squares or a stepped appearance). The resolution required for viewing the image on your computer monitor is less than what is needed for printing, typically 72ppi at the exact size you want the image to appear onscreen.

Two universal file formats used for digital photographs are TIFF and JPG. JPG format compresses data, resulting in a small file size commonly used for e-mailing images and onscreen viewing. There are several levels of compression you can apply when saving an image as a JPG, medium or high being your best compromise for quality and smaller file size. JPG compression results in some data loss and each time the file is resaved as a JPG, the image quality is reduced.

The TIFF format is a good choice for larger files (for print/publication) or for archiving images while retaining high quality. Both TIFF and JPG files are easily opened by any computer.

Generally when shooting with a digicam for maximum quality, select the highest resolution, usually a JPG format. When processing the file later using Photoshop, resample down to improve the result even more. Save the file as a TIFF and from this "master" file you can make duplicates as needed (small JPGs for e-mail).

What is the end use of the photos? Most galleries want 35 mm slides to review an artist's work, though digital files are a growing trend, with more galleries requesting initial submissions as e-mailed images and more artists/galleries selling art on the Web. If you need prints, they can be made from color slides, negatives, or digital files. Use a professional lab and foster a good working relationship with them. The copy service that some professional labs offer is worth investigating for small scale work.

Tips for Successful Photography

Light and Color Temperature

The color quality of light sources varies widely and is measured by a system that describes the color of the light as "color temperature" in degrees Kelvin. This is a numerical description, the lower numbers describing a redder light source (a candle is 1900°K) while higher numbers refer to bluer sources (skylight without direct sun is 11,000°K). Our eyes can adjust for these differences but films, especially slide films, will show color imbalances if shot with the wrong light source.

Basically there are two types of film—daylight rated for 5500°K and tungsten rated for 3200°K. Photographic tungsten light fixtures, like photofloods or quartz halogen lamps, have tungsten filaments that are designed to emit a specific color quality of light (3200°K) for use with tungsten films. So the best bet is to use tungsten film with tungsten sources and daylight film with natural outdoor light or flash for the most accurate color reproduction. If this is not possible and you have the wrong light source for your film, use a filter over the lens while shooting to correct the color.

These filters are called conversion filters and come in different strengths. An 80A or 80B blue filter will take out reddish yellow when daylight film is used with tungsten light correcting the imbalance. An 85B amber filter is used when tungsten film is shot in daylight illumination to remove excess blue. The color will be close to correct using a conversion filter. Don't forget to adjust exposure when using filters by 2/3 to two stops and consult the instructions that come with the filter.

Film

Use only 100-speed or slower professional film. My current recommendations for slide film are Fuji Provia for daylight or flash and Fuji RTP or Kodak EPY for tungsten light.

For print film use Fuji Reala or NPS for daylight and Fuji Reala with an 80B filter for tungsten. Don't degrade the quality of professional film by using an inexpensive filter or close up lens.

Lighting

Consider the type, size, quality, direction, and color temperature of your light source. All of these factors, as well as placement and diffusion of the light will influence the final result. Direct light on the artwork creates dark shadows with a distinct edge, especially if the source is small and/or far from the subject. Diffuse light is scattered light that seems to come from several directions, causing indistinct shadows, especially if the light source is large compared to your artwork.

Daylight Sources of Light

The color quality of natural sunlight is as varied as its brightness, making results inconsistent. Direct sun is rarely useful for photographing art due to its harsh shadows, while shooting in a shaded area results in a bluish color cast. On the other hand, diffusion of natu-

Light fixtures: studio electronic flash head, small handheld flash unit, photoflood tungsten lamp in reflector, quartz halogen photo/video fixture, halogen work light, quartz halogen studio lamp (Lowel).

Diffuse and direct light comparison. The photo on the left was taken with a diffuse (tent) light setup. Note the softer shadow and warmer color due to the diffusion material. The photo on the right was taken with mostly direct light. Notice the distinct shadow, cooler color, and more obvious texture. Vase by Peggy Elmes.

ral light is very desirable. Overcast days provide a lovely, even source of light akin to the soft boxes that photographers use. Use an 81A or 81B filter to warm up color if you are shooting slides in overcast conditions. Enclosing your artwork in a tent made of translucent white material can create an overcast effect on sunny days.

Blue bulbs are tungsten photofloods with a blue coating over the bulb. This coating alters its color balance so it can be used as a light source with daylight film without a filter. The blue coating on the bulb is like a blue filter on your lens. Personally, I have not found color results with these blue bulbs to be satisfactory, so do not recommend them.

The most expensive light source is a studio flash unit, which is used with daylight films. Unlike camera mounted flash units, pro flash heads have built-in tungsten lamps that allow a preview of the direction and quality of light. The flash generates far less heat than tungsten, which is a benefit if you are shooting museum artifacts or heat-sensitive art.

Tungsten Light Sources

Photoflood lamps use a screw-in tungsten filament 250/500 watt bulb that is mounted in a silver reflector.

For photo lighting, do not use household incandescent bulbs, as they are too red. Photofloods, rated for tungsten film, will go more reddish after six to eight hours of use, a concern if exact color is required. Quartz halogen lights made for photographic use are much more expensive than photofloods, however, the bulbs have a longer life and more consistent color balance. A cost-effective alternative to the expensive quartz halogen fixture is a halogen work light, sold in hardware stores. After purchasing a halogen work light, replace the existing bulb, which is somewhat yellowish, with a photographic bulb (FCZ) for perfect color and 300 hours of use, a very practical lighting solution for shooting tungsten slide film.

When working with lights, be aware of the fire potential—keep hot lights a safe distance away from flammable materials.

Controlling Light

Cajoling light into being where you want it to be, at a certain level of brightness, is what photographing art is all about. Photographers use custom accessories to control light, but you can accessorize with a minimal budget.

Aim for diffuse lighting. Create a diffusion tent

Tent lighting. Here, ripstop nylon was used to diffuse the main light from the top left for softer contrast. A black card was placed on the top rear area of the tent to block some light from reaching the background, creating a tonal graduation. The black tape lines on the studio floor indicate lights and camera positioning for copying flat art on the wall behind.

with translucent Plexiglass, ripstop nylon, drafting Mylar, or white polyester fabric stretched over a frame and placed in front of a light. This will transform a small light source into a larger one, providing even illumination that surrounds the subject.

Compare the effects with and without diffusion. Diffusion eliminates dark shadows and glare spots and the color quality will warm slightly, most noticeably on slide films. Another way to create diffusion is by using large white boards, white walls, or foam core sheets as reflectors. Direct the light(s) at the white surface, which will reflect a broad soft quality of light onto your set.

Direct light. This shot was taken using one main light pointed directly at the basket without diffusion or a reflector to soften the contrast. Note the distinct dark shadows and harsh appearance.

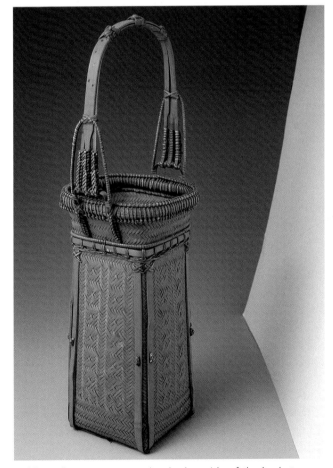

White reflectors even out the shadow side of the basket, revealing detail there, for a more balanced effect. This was shot with a tent lighting setup.

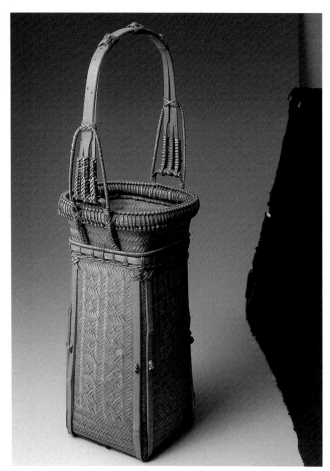

Black reflectors block all light from reaching the shadow side.

Silver reflectors add more brilliance to the shadow side for increased texture and detail, mimicking the effect of an additional light source without the resulting shadow.

This setup is ideal for large works of art, especially those with glossy surfaces (soapstone sculptures or varnished paintings). The walls of my studio are painted a very light neutral gray to facilitate this bounced lighting technique.

Diffusing or reflecting light reduces the overall subject contrast to a level where the photograph will show good detail in both the highlight and shadow areas of the artwork.

Sometimes a combination of direct and diffuse light is needed to reveal texture and emphasize volume. Be careful when adding additional lights—if used directly they can create artificial-looking double shadows.

The direction of light becomes obvious if you note where the shadows are falling. Light coming from on or near the camera shows less texture, flattens the form, and often results in hot spots on the object. For a more natural look, position the light at a 45° angle above and to one side of your diffusion tent, then use reflectors on the opposite side and in front if necessary to lighten shadows.

Reflectors

Reflectors are used to reflect light from the main source back onto the object, usually to brighten an area that is too dark. You can make reflectors from white material such as foam core or matt board, or, for even more brilliance, try silver foil matt board, tin foil, or small mirrors. Use neutral colored reflectors unless you want to introduce color into your shot (gold foil boards and nutmeg-colored paper will warm up the result). Sometimes black cards are used instead of white for a darkening effect to subdue reflections of a light background onto a black glazed pot, for example.

Positioning reflectors can be challenging. Start by placing the reflector directly opposite your main light as close to the piece as possible, checking to see that it does not show in your camera viewfinder. Move it around and tip it up or down slightly while studying the lightening effect it is having on your artwork. Remove it completely, then quickly reposition it again, noting the effect once more. Your eyes and careful observation will decide the best placement. Clamp or tape the reflector securely into position.

Light Direction

Consider the direction light is coming from and how that influences the look of your art. Diffuse light from above works for many objects, especially pottery. Use white or black reflectors on the sides and/or in front, depending on what looks best. Blocking light is an often overlooked control. Black opaque cards can be used to prevent light from spilling onto a background. With careful positioning, you can create subtle background gradations from light to dark. Increasing the distance from the subject to the background makes getting gradation easier, since the light intensity will naturally drop off if the background is three to six feet away. Cutting the edge of your black blocking card in a sawtooth pattern will help soften the transition zone, avoiding an abrupt change from light to dark.

Another possibility is to position the light source above and behind the object, with large reflectors in front of the piece for a soft, even quality overall and clearly defined edges. This is ideal for reflective pieces such as polished sculptural work or bronzes that would show hot spots from the lights if shot using frontal

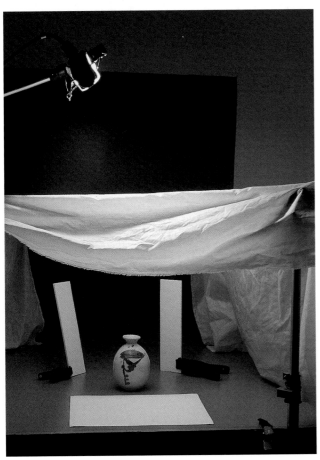

Overhead light diffused with ripstop nylon and white reflectors placed around the vase to brighten and give edge highlights. The background gradation to black is easier to achieve on this set with the increased distance of the subject to the background.

lighting. Backlighting can also be used successfully for translucent or glass objects.

Check the front of your lens to make sure no light is hitting it directly, especially if using backlighting. If this is happening, use a lens hood (lens shade) that screws on the front of your lens (the hood must be the right size for its focal length). A lens hood prevents unwanted light from hitting the front of the lens directly, which causes flare and results in a loss of contrast in the image. The effect is similar to what you see while driving into the sun without the car visor shading your eyes. Metal lens hoods are more useful than rubber ones, especially if your lens gets dropped (the metal hood could take the damage instead of your lens). Along with a lens hood, you may also need to position black cards between the light and lens, just out of frame, to block a potential flare situation, which is the ruin of many a fine photo.

Backgrounds

When preparing for a photo shoot, first inspect and dust your artwork, then place it on a clean background. When choosing a background, think in complementary terms (place a light object on a dark background and vise versa). Don't overpower the art with flashy colors or busy backgrounds—keep it simple. You can buy rolls of seamless paper from photo suppliers. These are handy but expensive and fragile. They are also slightly textured. Laminates like Formica or Arborite are more functional and durable than paper. Check local building supply stores for 4 by 8 foot or 2 by 4 foot sheets. These are washable too! Remember neutral colors are best. Clamp one edge of the laminate background to a table and run the length up a wall for a smooth, untextured cove background. If you are using laminates, tape all four edges of the sheet for easier handling and safety. Before placing an artwork on any background, tape or otherwise cover the rough bottom so it won't scratch the surface.

Some fabrics make suitable backgrounds too. Black velvet eliminates shadows and gives the artwork a floating quality. When using velvet, position the fabric nap toward the light for a maximum black effect. Velvet is not great for close-ups due to the heavy texture in the fabric nap. On velvet, shadows disappear but so will the dark edges of the piece. If your camera allows, use the depth of field preview to stop the lens down to f16 and look through the viewfinder. The image will look dark, making it more obvious where the problem areas are; reflectors or a lighter background will help.

Other useful backgrounds are clay or slate tiles (great for jewelry and other small objects), handmade paper, black Plexiglass or white Plexiglass lit from below.

Photographing Flat Art

When photographing flat art using tungsten lights (see the illustration), block out all the daylight illumination and use tape to mark lines on the floor to indicate positioning for the lights and camera. Use two 500-watt tungsten bulbs positioned at a 45° angle to the art. If some glare shows on the edges, move the lights to a 30° angle, hang the art vertically rather than horizontally, or use a longer lens to get farther back, all of which will reduce the glare problem. Center the camera on a tripod , using a 50 to 135 mm lens. A long carpenter's level can be used to ensure that the camera back is parallel to the shooting wall. A viewing screen with a grid is also a useful accessory for centering and squaring. Position two black cards at the front sides of the camera to keep direct light off the lens. The meter readings from a gray card (or incident meter) should be within 1/3 stop across the art. Bracket exposures when shooting slides and include control patches/gray scale beside the art if it's for reproduction.

If the art is behind glass, use a black cloth or card twice the size of the art in front of the camera with a hole cut for the lens. This will eliminate all reflections into the glass.

To light flat art to show texture (see the illustration), one light is pointed at the opposite edge of the art and bounces off a large white board that fills in the shadows and evens out the side-to-side exposure reading to within 1/3 stop. Position a black card on the same side as the light fixture to block light from hitting the lens. If you are shooting slides, bracket the exposures for an exact result (not necessary with print films). If the piece is very large, stack a second light above the first one for more even lighting. Consider from what direction the light looks best and hang the piece accordingly (the slide can be rotated later for viewing).

I shoot most flat art on a black velvet background to avoid having to mask off the edges of the slide with foil tape. For stretched or framed pieces, use a nail behind the velvet for hanging. For works on paper or unframed art, use T-pins or push pins.

Another way of dealing with unframed works is to shoot down on them or set up a piece of plywood at about 30° angle on the floor. Cover the plywood with velvet and lay the artwork on top, then position your camera back parallel for shooting. You might be able to use a painter's easel instead of plywood to hold the piece.

Exposure

An exposure meter measures the quantity of light and translates that into a "meter reading." which is a combination of time (shutter speed) and amount

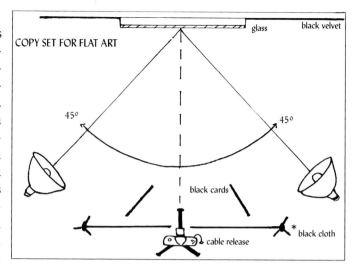

When photographing flat art using tungsten lights, place the elements as shown.

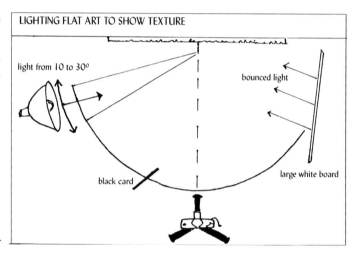

To show the texture of a flat piece, place the elements as shown.

(aperture). The aperture is a varying size hole inside the lens that lets in more (f4) or less (f22) light (think of f-stop numbers as fractions). The combination of shutter speed and aperture influences how much light is allowed to reach the film, determining the density (darkness or lightness) of the photograph.

There are two types of light meters—incident and reflected. A reflected meter measures the light reflected from the subject, while an incident meter measures light falling on the subject. The meters built into cameras are the reflected type.

All meters are calibrated to read and reproduce a medium 18% gray tone no matter what tone your subject is, so use a gray card to take the exposure reading if you are using a reflected meter or your camera meter. Position the gray card so it is in the same light and plane as the artwork, and move the camera (or handheld reflected light meter) in close to fill the viewfinder with the gray card. It doesn't need to be in focus to take the reading—just watch that you don't cast a shadow on the card while metering. If you use the exposure taken from the gray card with a reflected meter, gray will come out gray, white will be white, and all subject tones should end up being the right density. This is not the case if you are metering off a subject comprised of mostly all dark or all light tones with a reflected meter. The meter is fooled and makes both subjects look grayish.

Incident meters work differently in that they read the light falling on the subject and therefore do not take into account subject tonality. Their white plastic dome is like a built-in gray card. They are useful for taking quick multiple readings across a large subject area to determine if the lighting is even. Point the dome of your incident meter toward the camera from the subject position so that it is receiving the same light as the subject. A gray card is not needed with incident meters.

Getting the correct exposure is critical with slide film, because a 1/2 stop change in the aperture setting (f-stop) makes a slide noticeably darker or lighter. With slide film, bracketing (varying the exposure setting by changing the f-stop) is advisable. Print films are not so critical, since this difference can be compensated for in the printing stage.

When shooting artwork it is essential to use a sturdy tripod with a cable release to eliminate blurry photos at slow shutter speeds. Slow shutter speeds like 1/2 second will allow the use of smaller apertures (f11 to f32), which give more depth of focus. For flat art, try f8 to f11, for three-dimensional sculpture use f11 to f32, and for jewelry or close-ups use f22 to f45. If your lens has a depth-of-field scale, consult the camera manual on its use or try to focus about 1/3 of the way into the subject depth for best sharpness throughout the piece.

Testing the Lighting

Before shooting a lot of slides in the same light setup, do a test series. Use an "average" subject that is not too dark or too light. For the first shot, use the meter reading from the gray card at your chosen aperture to equal a normal exposure. You will have to adjust the shutter speed until your meter indicates that this is a correct reading. Leave your shutter speed at this normal setting for the next four shots.

Shot #2: open up 1/2 stop using the lens aperture (set lens halfway between f-stops)

Shot #3: open up one stop from the normal exposure (f11 if normal is f16)

Shot #4: close down 1/2 stop from the normal exposure

Shot #5: close down one stop from the normal reading (f22 if normal is f16)

These five different exposures (a bracketed set) will indicate which exposure is best and the quality of color you will get using this same light/camera setup in the future. A professional lab can "clip test" these first five frames and return the rest of the unexposed roll for you to shoot later. Take detailed notes of the variables (camera, lens, film, exposure, lighting, diffusion material) to ensure that results are repeatable. Include a lighting diagram with measurements.

Color Management

Color management is a huge issue in photography and it becomes even more complex in the digital realm. Many variables affect color balance in every step of the process. One way to calibrate color is to include Kodak's Color Control Patches/ Gray Scale in your shot or at least in the first frame. Control patches and gray scale are standard industry references to measure color and

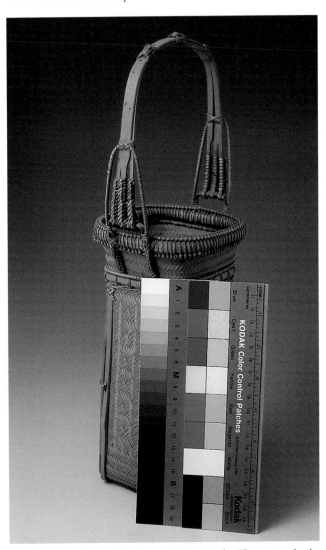

Kodak Color Control Patches and Gray Scale. These standard references indicate good color balance and the exposure achieved with the combination of film, lighting, diffusion, and exposure used for this shot.

Detail shot. This close-up clearly shows the construction, glaze, color, and textural quality of this vessel by Judy Weeden. These qualities would be difficult to see in an overall shot.

correct exposure. Gray cards can also be used but are not as informative. Designers and printers can adjust your prints so that colors are accurate using these known references.

Film does have limitations—certain colors will not reproduce exactly as we see them yet may respond to a different choice of film or being shot digitally. Again, testing is necessary to determine this.

Looking Professional

The final touches will give your presentation a professional edge. Label slides and prints. Include both detail and overall shots of your work. Get a portfolio case or slide presentation pages for your photos and arrange them in a clean, simple format that is easy to view. For long-term storage, use archival pages and metal boxes.

Employ a professional to design and output your brochures or other promotional material. You invest a lot in your art, so it's more than worthwhile to carry the quality through to the very end.

Janet Dwyer, 234 Fairway Crescent, Salt Spring Island, British Columbia, Canada V8K 1M6, e-mail: jdwyer@saltspring.com.

Conclusion

In compiling this book, I hope to have given the reader the benefit of a huge amount of varied experiences in the field. Some will relate to you, others won't. I was fortunate to have parents who were in business and I learned how business works from an early age. The process became almost intuitive when I started my own studio. Now, over 50 years since I sold my first artwork, I feel well equipped to offer some advice to others at different stages of their artistic careers. It comes in the form or do's and don'ts, in no particular order of priority.

Don'ts

- Don't overextend yourself—know your limits.
- Don't be afraid to take on help—free yourself for what you do best.
- Don't get stuck in the rut of producing the same old thing—the work becomes tired, the artist bored, the customer disinterested, and the reputation diminished.
- Don't overextend your budget without knowing where the money is coming from.
- Don't be afraid to explore and take risks in the development of your work.
- Don't oversell yourself—bombastic sales pitches are likely to produce negative results.
- Don't miss any opportunity to learn more about your art—it liberates.
- Don't underestimate your customers or clients—they are your living.
- Don't overspend on realizing the "perfect" studio—prove yourself first.
- Don't compromise your work for any reason.
- Don't plagiarize other people's work or style—someone out there will know and it will always come back to haunt you.

Do's

- Do develop a strong work ethic and the motivation to succeed.
- Do produce the best work that you possibly can—you never know who might see it.
- Do stand behind your product—a dissatisfied customer can do you a lot of damage.
- Do be positive—the world is full of potential customers for your work.
- Do be reliable—if you say that you are going to be open from 10 to 5 daily, then be there. Unreliability creates a bad reflection on artists who are reliable.
- Do get as good an education as possible before turning professional, either through college or apprenticeship if you can find one. The more you know, the more options you have.
- Do check local bylaws to make sure you can do what you want to do, where you want to do it.
- Do help others in need—not only does it feel good, it pays great returns.
- Do participate in organizations related to your medium—they are a great source of like-minded people with much information to share.
- Do volunteer in organizations—they don't run themselves.
- Do take care of your health, body, and mind—most arts are physically and mentally demanding.
- Do take time for yourself to rejuvenate and re-energize.
- Do take time for family and friends—they are your safety net.
- Do remember the child within—he or she needs nourishment and love.
- Do keep growing in your work—it keeps clients interested and your mind active.
- Do save money where possible.
- Do remember that a potter's best friend is a hammer.

Developing and living the lifestyle of a self-employed creative artist is the most satisfying that I can imagine. Sometimes it is tough and challenging, often impecunious, incredibly variable, sometimes very busy, sometimes hopelessly romantic, occasionally high-powered, free of much that grates in today's society, self-enabling, and very, very much envied.

Good luck in your search, your journey, and your success.

About the Author

Robin Hopper is an internationally recognized ceramic artist, author, educator, consultant, and garden designer. Born in London, England, and trained there at Croydon College of Art, he has been working as an artist since 1955. Primarily a studio potter, he has developed studios in both England and Canada, and has working experience on four continents. He now makes his home on an island off the west coast of Canada. He is the author of *The Ceramic Spectrum*, and *Functional Pottery*, and recently updated and expanded the third edition of *Clay and Glazes for the Potter* by the late Daniel Rhodes. He is currently working on a new book *Making Marks: Discovering the Decorated Ceramic Surface*, to be published by Krause Publications in 2004.

Bibliography and Resources

Books, Publications, and Directories

Art and Fear, by David Bayles and Ted Orland. Santa Barbara, CA, Capra Press, 1994. www.amazon.com

Art and Reality: The New Standard Reference Guide and Business Plan for Actively Developing Your Career as an Artist, by Robert J. Abbott. Santa Ana, CA, Seven Locks Press, 1997. www.pma-online.org

Art Information and the Internet: How to Find It, How to Use It, by Lois Swan. Phoenix, AZ, The Oryx Press, 1998. www.oryxpress.com

Art Law: The Guide for Collectors, Investors Dealers and Artists, by Ralph E. Lerner and Judith Bresler. Practicing Law Institute, New York, NY, revised 1998.

Art Marketing Sourcebook, ArtNetwork, Nevada City, CA, regularly revised. www.artmarketing.com

Artist Beware, by Michael McCann. The Lyons Press, New York, revised 2001. www.lyonspress.com

Business Entities for Artists Fact Sheet, by Mark Quail. Available from Artists' Legal Advice Services and Canadian Artists' Representation Ontario (CARO), Toronto, Ontario, 1991. www.carfacontarion.ca

Business Information Folder, Ontario Crafts Council, Toronto, Ontario, Canada, revised annually. www.craft.on.ca

Crafting as a Business, by Wendy Rosen. Published by The Rosen Group. Distributed by Sterling Publishing Company.

Creating a Life Worth Living, by Carol Lloyd, Harper Perennial, New York, 1997. www.harpercollins.com

Directory of Minority Arts Organizations, edited by Carol Ann Huston. Office of Civil Rights, National Endowment for the Arts, Washington, DC. www.arts.endow.gov/learn/civil.html

Directory of the Arts, Canadian Conference of the Arts, Ottawa, Ontario, Canada, revised 2000. www.ffa.ucalgary.ca

Estate Planning for Artists, by Ruth J. Waters, Marcee Yeager and Paul Barulich, Women's Caucus for Art, 1992. Available from Ruth J. Waters, e-mail: rjwaters@sirius.com

Fear of Filing: A Beginner's Guide to Tax Preparation and Record Keeping for Artists, Performers, Writers and Freelance Professionals, by Theodore W. Striggles and Barbara Sieck Taylor. Volunteer Lawyers for the Arts, New York, NY, revised 1985. www.vlany.org

Getting Funded: A Complete Guide to Proposal Writing, by Mary Stewart Hall. Continuing Education Press, School of Extended Studies, Portland State University, Portland, OR, revised regularly. www.cep.pdx.edu

Guide to Canadian Arts Grants, Canada Grant Service, Toronto, Ontario, Canada, regularly revised. www.interlog.com/~cgs

Keeping Clay Work Safe and Legal, National Council of Education on the Ceramic Arts, revised 1996. www.caseweb.com/acts

Legal Guide for the Visual Artist, by Tad Crawford. Allworth Press, New York, revised 1999. www.allworth.com

Manitoba Visual Artists Index, CARFAC Manitoba, Winnipeg, Manitoba, Canada. www.umanitoba.ca/schools/art/gallery/hpgs/carfac

Selling Art on the Internet, by Marques Vickers. Vallejo, CA, 2000. www.marquesv.com

Selling Your Crafts, by Susan Joy Sager. Allworth Press, New York, 1998. www.allworth.com

Thank You for Being Such a Pain: Spiritual Guidance for Dealing with Difficult People, by Mark I. Rosen. Three Rivers Press, New York, 1998. www.random-house.com

The Artist in Business: Basic Business Practices, by Craig Dreesen. Arts Extension Service Division of Continuing Education, University of Massachusetts, Amherst, MA, revised 1996. www.umass.edu/aes

The Artist's Guide to New Markets: Opportunities to Show and Sell Art Beyond Galleries, by Peggy Hadden. Allworth Press, New York, 1998. www.allworth.com

The Artist's Survival Manual: A Complete Guide to Marketing Your Work, by Toby Judith Klayman with Cobbett Steinberg. Originally published by Charles Scribner's Sons, now published by Toby Judith Klayman and Joseph Branchcomb, revised in 1996. www.calawyersforthearts.org

The Artist-Gallery Partnership: A Practical Guide to Consigning Art, by Tad Crawford and Susan Mellon. Allworth Press, New York, revised 1998. www.allworth.com

The Business of Art, edited by Lee Caplin. Prentice-Hall Direct, Englewood Cliffs, NJ, revised 2000. www.phdirect.com

The International Directory of Corporate Art Collections, edited by S. R. Howarth. International Art Alliance, Inc., Largo, FL, revised 2000. www.exhibitionsonline.org

The Tax Workbook for Artists and Others, by Susan Harvey Dawson, ArtBusiness, Inc., Alexandria, VA, revised annually.

Organizations

Alberta Craft Council, 10106 124th St., Edmonton, Alberta T5N 1P6, Canada, 403-488-6611, e-mail: acc@campsumart.ab.ca. www.albertacraft.ab.ca

American Craft Council, 72 Spring St., New York, NY 10012-4006, 212-274-0630, www.craftcouncil.org

American Federation of Arts, 41 E. 65th St., New York, NY 10021, 215-988-7700, www.afaweb.org

American Needlepoint Guild, Ann Caswel, 34 Valley Creek Circle, Middleton, WI 53562-1990, 608-831-3228, www.needlepoint.org

American Quilter's Society, Helen Squire, POB 3290, Paducah, KY 42002-3290, 270-898-7903, www.aqsquilt.com

American Sculptors and Casters Association (ASCA), 8 Ecclestone, Irvine, CA 92604.

American Society of Furniture Artists (ASOFA), Box 35339, Houston, TX 77235-7600, 713-721-7600.

Americans for the Arts, 1000 Vermont Ave. NW, 12th Floor, Washington, DC 20005, and 1 East 53rd St., New York, NY 10022. www.artsusa.org

Archie Bray Foundation, 2915 Country Club Ave., Helena, MT 59602, 406-443-3502, www.archiebray.org

Art Alliance for Contemporary Glass, 624 Central St., Evanston, IL 60201, 847-869-1163, www.ContempGlass.org

Art Dealers Association of America, 575 Madison Ave., New York, NY 10022. 212-940-8925, www.artdealers.org

Artist Help Network, www.artisthelpnetwork.com

Arts & Business Council, 200 South Broad St., #700, Philadelphia, PA 19102-3896, 215-790-3620, e-mail: arts&biz@gpcc.com

Baltimore Clayworks, 5707 Smith Ave., Baltimore, MD 21209, 410-578-1919, www.baltimoreclayworks.org

Canada Council for the Arts, POB1047, Ottawa, Ontario, Canada K1P 5V8, www.canadacouncil.ca

Canadian Craft Federation (formerly Canadian Crafts Council), c/o Ontario Crafts Council, Designer's Walk, 170 Bedford Road, #300, Toronto, Ontario, Canada M5R 2K9, www.canadiancraftsfederation.ca

CARFAC National, 401 Richmond St., Suite 442, Toronto, Ontario, Canada M5V 3A8, www.carfac.ca

Clay Studio, 139 North Second St., Philadelphia, PA 19106, 215-925-3453 ext 13, www.libertynet.org/~claystdo

Craft Emergency Relief Fund (CERF), Cornelia Carey, POB 838, Montpelier, VT 05601, 802-229-2306, www.craftemergency.org

Crafts Association of British Columbia, 1386 Cartwrite St., Granville Island, Vancouver, B.C., Canada, www.cabc.net

Enamalist Society, Tom Ellis, POB 310, Newport, KY 41072, 606-291-3800.

Glass Art Society (GAS), Penny Berk, 1305 4th Ave., #711, Seattle, WA 98101-2401, 206-382-1305, www.glassart.org

Handweavers Guild of America, Inc., Two Executive Concourse, Suite 201, 3327 Duluth Highway, Duluth, GA 30096-3301, www.weavespindye.org

Harbourfront Craft Studio, Melanie Egan, 235 Queens Quay West, Toronto, Ontario, Canada M5J 2G8, 416-973-4963, www.harbourfront.on.ca

Int'l Gemological Institute (GIA), 589 5th Ave., New York, NY 10017, 212-753-7100, www.igi-usa.com

Int'l Association of Fine Art Digital Printmakers, 570 Higuera St., Suite 120, San Luis Obispo, CA 93401, www.iafadp.org

John Michael Kohler Arts Center, Karen Kohler, 608 New York Ave., Sheboygan, WI 53081, 414-452-8602.

Manitoba Crafts Council, 237 McDermot Ave., Winnipeg, Manitoba, Canada R3B 0S4, 204-947-0340, www.craftspace.org

Minnesota Crafts Council, Dave Glenn, 528 Hennepin Ave. #216, Minneapolis, MN 55403, 612-333-7789, www.mtn.org/mncraft

Museum Reference Center, Smithsonian Institution Libraries, Office of Museum Studies, Arts and Industries Building, Room 2235, 900 Jefferson Dr. SW, Washington, DC 20560-0427, www.sil.si.edu/branches

National Conference on Artists, Michigan Chapter, 216 Fisher Bldg., 3011 West Grand Blvd., Detroit, MI 48202-3096, www.ncamich.org

National Council Edu Ceramic Arts (NCECA), Regina Brown, POB 1677, Brandon, OR 97411, 514-347-7505, www.nceca.net

National Quilting Association, 8510 High Ridge Rd.,
  Ellicott City, MD 21043-0393, 410-461-5733,
  www.nqaquilts.org

Newfoundland & Labrador Crafts Dev. Assn., Devon
  House, 59 Duckworth St., St. John's, Newfoundland,
  Canada A1C 1E6, 709-753-2749.
  www.craftcouncil.nf.ca

Ontario Crafts Council, Designers Walk, 170 Bedford
  Rd., Toronto, Ontario, Canada M5R 2K9,
  www.craft.on.ca

PEI Crafts Council, 156 Richmond St., Charlottetown,
  PEI, Canada C1A 1H9, 902-892-5152,
  www.peicraftscouncil.com

Pennsylvania Guild of Craftsmen, 10 Stable Mill Trail,
  Richboro, PA 18954-1702, 814-504-5538,
  www.pennsylvaniacrafts.com

Potters for Peace, 610 Livermore St., Yellow Springs,
  OH 45387, 303-377-7998, www.potpaz.org

Quebec Craft Council/Conseil D'art, Denise Poirier, 350
  St. Paul est, #400, Montreal, Quebec H2Y 1H2, 514-
  861-2787, www.metiers-d'art.qc.ca

Saskatchewan Crafts Council, 813 Broadway Ave.,
  Saskatoon, Saskatchewan, Canada S7N 1B5,
  www.saskcraftcouncil.org

South Dakota Arts Council, 800 Govenors Dr., Pierre,
  SD 57501, 605-773-3131, www.sdarts.org

Southwest Craft Center, Ric Collier, 300 Augusta, San
  Antonio, TX 78205, 512-224-1848.

Surface Design Association, POB 360, Sebastopol, CA
  95473-0360, www.surfacedesign.org

Texas Art Commission, Betty Swizer, POB 13406,
  Austin, TX 78711, 512-463-5535,
  www.arts.state.tx.us

Texas Visual Arts Association, 2207 Spanish Trail,
  Arlington, TX 76013, 817-461-1525.

The American Ceramic Society, POB 6136, Westerville,
  OH 43086-6136, www.ceramics.org

The Crafts Council, 44a Pentonville Rd., London N1
  9BY, England, www.craftscouncil.org.uk

The Studio Potter, POB 70, Goffstown, NH 03045,
  www.studiopotter.org

Vermont State Craft Center, Frog Hollow, 1 Mill St.,
  Middlebury, VT 05753, 802-388-3177, www.froghol-
  low.org

Visual Arts Ontario, 1153A Queen St. West, Toronto,
  Ontario, Canada M6J 1J4, www.vao.org

Watershed Center for the Ceramic Arts, Lynn Gibson,
  19 Brickhill Rd., Newcastle, ME 04553, 207-882-
  6075, www.watershedcenterceramicarts.org

Western States Arts Federation (WESTAF), 1543
  Champa St., Ste. 220, Denver, CO 80202, www.west-
  af.org

World Crafts Council (WCC), International Secretariat,
  Anthrakitou 5 & Tsechouli St., Kastro Ioanninon,
  Ioannina, GR45 221, Greece, www.wccwis.gr

Magazines and Periodicals

American Craft Magazine, 72 Spring St., New York, NY
  10012-4019, 212-274-0630,
  www.Council@Craftcouncil.org

American Glass Review, POB 2147, Clifton, NJ 07015-
  2147, 973-779-1600.

American Woodworker Magazine, 33 East Minor St.,
  Emmaus, PA 18098-00001, 610-967-8029,
  www.Americanwoodworker.com

AmericanStyle Magazine, 3000 Chestnut Ave., Ste. 304,
  Baltimore, MD 21211, 410-235-5116, www.ameri-
  canstyle.com

Art and Auction, ArtPress International, 11 East 36th
  St., 9th Floor, New York, NY 10016-3318,
  www.artandauction.com

Art in America, 575 Broadway, 5th Floor, New York,
  NY 10012, 212-941-2800.

Art Matters, POB 1628, Fort Washington, PA 19034,
  www.philly-art-world.com

Artforum, 65 Bleecker St., New York, NY 10012-2466,
  212-475-4000.

ARTnews, 48 West 38th St., New York, NY 10018-6211,
  212-398-1690, www.artnewsonline.com

Ceramics Monthly, American Ceramics Society, POB
  6136, Westerville, OH 43086-6136, www.ceramic-
  smonthly.com

Ceramics Review, Ceramic Review Publishing Ltd., 25
  Foubert's Place, London W1F 7QF, England,
  www.ceramic-review.com

Ceramics: Art and Perception, 35 William St.,
  Paddington, Sydney NSW 2021, Australia,
  www.ceramicart.com.au

*Clay Times: The Journal of Ceramics, Trends and
  Techniques*, POB 365, Waterford, VA 20197,
  www.claytimes.com

Clayart Magazine, e-mail: clayart@lsv.ceramics.org

FiberArts Magazine, 50 College St., Asheville, NC
  28801, 704-253-0467, www.larkbooks.com

Fine Woodworking Magazine, POB 5506, Newtown, CT
  06470, 203-426-8171. www.taunton.com

Glass Art Magazine, POB 260377, Highlands Ranch,
  CO 80126, 303-791-8998.

Glass Craftsman Magazine, POB 678, Richboro, PA
  18954, 215-860-9947, www.artglassworld.com

Glass, The Urban Glass Art Journal, 647 Fulton St.,
  Brooklyn, NJ 11217, 718-625-3685.

Interior Design Magazine, 249 West 17th St., New York,
  NY 10016, 212-645-0067, www.interiordesign.net

Metalsmith Magazine, 5009 Londonderry Dr., Tampa, FL 33647, 813-977-5326.

Metropolis Magazine, 177 East 87th St., New York, NY 10028, 212-722-5050, www.metropolismag.com

NICHE Magazine, 3000 Chestnut Ave., Ste. 304, Baltimore, MD 21211, 410-889-3093, www.americancraft.com

Ornament Magazine, POB 2349, San Marcos, CA 92079, 760-599-0222.

Pottery Making Illustrated, POB 6136, Westerville, OH 43086-6136, 614-794-5809, www.potterymaking.org

Shuttle Spindle & Dyepot, Handweavers Guild of America, 3327 Duluth Hwy, #201, Duluth, MN 30136-3373, www.weavespindye.org

Stained Glass, 6 South West 2nd St., Ste. 7, Lee's Summit, MO 64063, 800-438-9581, www.artglassworld.com/mag/sglass/sglass.html

The Crafts Report, PO 1992, Wilmington, DE 19899, 302-656-2209, www.craftsreport.com

Threads Magazine, 63 South Main St., Newtown, CT 06470, 203-426-8171.

Software

QuickBooks. www.quickbooks.com

Miscellaneous

Mint Museum of Craft & Design Shop, 2730 Randolph Rd., Charlotte, NC 28207, 704-337-2000, www.mintmuseum.org

Out of Hand, 6166 North Scottsdale Rd., #502, Scottsdale, AZ 85250, Karen Kline, 602-998-0977.

Professional Services

Artists Rights Society, 536 Broadway, 5th Floor, New York, NY 10012, 212-420-9160, www.arsny.com

Business Volunteers for the Arts, 410 Eighth St. NW, #600, Washington, DC 20004, 202-638-2406, www.fine-art.com/org/bva.html

Center for Small Business Development, 35 Claremont Ave., Babylon, NY 11703, 516-661-5181.

The Rosen Group, 3000 Chestnut Ave. #304, Baltimore, MD 21211, 410-889-2933, www.americancraft.com

More References
by Robin Hopper

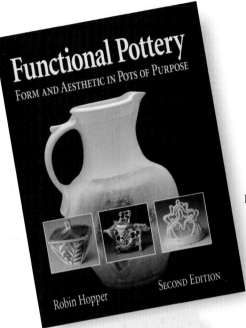

Functional Pottery
Form and Aesthetic in Pots of Purpose, Second Edition
by Robin Hopper

Reading through this new edition of Functional Pottery is like having a ceramic museum, art gallery, encyclopedia, and master potter at your side to teach and inspire you. This revised and expanded work is one of the most beautiful and informative books on pottery design and pottery making ever produced. With more than 250 color photographs of both historical and contemporary pottery, along with scores of black and white photographs and drawings, author Robin Hopper teaches the "why" as well as the "how to" of functional pottery design.

Softcover • 8¼ x 10⅞ • 256 pages
300 b&w photos • 250 color photos
Item# FPOT2 • $44.95

Clay and Glazes for the Potter
Third Edition
by Daniel Rhodes, Revised and Expanded by Robin Hopper

This revised and expanded edition of Daniel Rhodes' seminal book on fundamentals of ceramic technology adheres closely to editions published in 1957 and revised in 1973. Updated and simplified where necessary, with additional sections devoted to health hazards, computer calculation programs, increased color information, and expanded photographic images of both historical and contemporary work. Over 250 color photos plus illustrations and charts offer detailed information for today's potter.

Softcover • 8¼ x 10⅞ • 352 pages • 250 color photos
Item# CGFP3 • $39.95

The Ceramic Spectrum
A Simplified Approach to Glaze & Color Development, Second Edition
by Robin Hopper

Author Robin Hopper brings 45 years of experience and education to his new edition of this ceramist's staple. With easy to follow and understand directions, accompanied by photos, charts and drawings, covering Egyptian pastes, high texture glazes and flux variation triaxial, among other topics, this is a must-have for any ceramist or potter.

Softcover • 8¼ x 10⅞ • 256 pages • 300 color photos
Item# CESP2 • $44.95

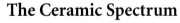

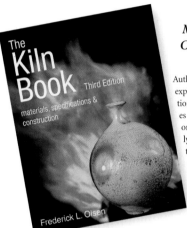

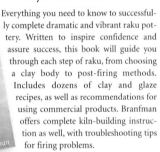